Is There A Stone In Your Soul You Can't Shake Loose?

In our quest to win freedom from the ties that bind, we spend most of our lives struggling to overcome vague foes that fade in and out, like the shadows that move across the forest floor each time the sun moves behind a cloud.

Yet, for all of the battles engaged and won, for all the changes we've made in our lifestyles and relationships, one thing remains basically the same. We still feel tied down! There's a stone in our soul we can't shake loose.

To satisfy our longing to live the way we want, Guy Finley says we need to become aware of one thing: *blaming any exterior condition in our lives as the culprit behind our feeling tied down or captive is like getting angry at our shoes for being laced too tight!*

No one but you controls the way you think, feel, and respond to external events, which means the responsibility for freeing yourself from self punishing patterns must begin with you. But how can you bridge the gap between realizing that Truth and actually learning to use it to pursue something Higher, something happier?

That's where the simple yet brilliant insights in *Freedom From The Ties that Bind* come into play. This book isn't about settling for a better way to live the life you're living now—it's about living another kind of life altogether. It's about transforming your *inner* life, which is the only way to make any real change in your *outer* life. It's about learning how to live in a bright and brand-new world, everyday, where your greatest pleasure is the natural procession of your own life's events.

There really is a realm where such wholeness rules—and it's inside of *you. Freedom From The Ties That Bind* shows the way into this realm and, upon entering it, the ultimate secret of self liberation: *you already are everything you've ever wanted to be.*

ABOUT THE AUTHOR

Guy Finley has enjoyed numerous successful careers, including composing award-winning music for many popular recording artists, motion pictures, and television programs. From 1970 through 1979, he wrote and recorded his own albums for the prestigious Motown and RCA record labels. Guy is the son of late-night talk show pioneer and radio celebrity Larry Finley.

In 1980, after travels to India and parts of the Far East in search of Truth and Higher Wisdom, Guy voluntarily retired from his flourishing career in order to simplify his life and continue with his inner studies.

Books and books-on-tape by Guy Finley include *The Secret of Letting Go*, *The Secret Way of Wonder*, *The Power of a Free Mind*, and *The Keys of Kings*.

Freedom From The Ties That Bind

The Secret Of Self Liberation

Guy Finley

1997
Llewellyn Publications
St. Paul, Minnesota 55164-0383, U.S.A.

FIRST EDITION
Fifth Printing, 1997

Library of Congress Cataloging-in-Publication Data
Finley, Guy, 1949–
    Freedom from the ties that bind : the secret of self liberation/
  Guy Finley.
          p.   cm.
    ISBN 0-87542-217-9
    1. Self-actualization (Psychology). 2. Autonomy (Psychology).
  I. Title.
    BF637.S4F55   1994
    158—dc20   93-42181
                                                           CIP

Llewellyn Worldwide does not participate in, endorse, or have any authority or responsibility concerning private business transactions between our authors and the public.
    All mail addressed to the author is forwarded but the publisher cannot, unless specifically instructed by the author, give out an address or phone number.

Llewellyn Publications
A Division of Llewellyn Worldwide, Ltd.
P.O. 64383, St. Paul, MN 55164-0383

CONTENTS

Introduction

W HAT IF YOU KNEW THAT EVERYTHING WAS ALL RIGHT, right now? Isn't this what you really want? When you face the sun, the shadows are at your back, so what if the only reason your life isn't going as well as you would like is because you've been searching for the sunrise while facing west?!

Why are you reading this very book now? Isn't it because your heart tells you there's still something new you need to learn and understand? If you're like me, you've sampled the spectrum of self-help "solutions." I needn't list the multitude of books, tapes, seminars, programs, regimens, theories, and techniques I've tried (some are too embarrassing even to think back upon), but doesn't this insightful quote of Thoreau's sum it all up for you too? "Everything counts for gain when we are cosmically awake. Nothing counts, unless we are awake. No enjoyments last, no successes satisfy, no gains have meaning unless accomplished in a state of wakefulness."

I didn't have much of an understanding of what Thoreau meant by this when I first read it, but I sensed that it was accurate and that it applied to me. Something rang true about it. As I began to proceed in this new direction of what being awake implied, I discovered it was the mental equivalent of turning away from my old west-facing stance and toward the east where I then got my first glimpse of the sunrise. I actually began to *think differently*, and that was the beginning of an entirely new life for me.

Until you discover and seek this new understanding of your mind and its thoughts, nothing you do, as Thoreau said, will satisfy. But once you begin to think in this whole new way, nothing can keep your heart's desire from you. I'm not getting religious or pious on you here; this is a very practical principle I'm describing. "The rich get richer and the poor get poorer" is an absolutely true statement. Substitute any word you like for "rich" and that statement also will be factual. Try happy, content, wise, serene, strong ... All of these inner riches will be yours. "For everyone who has will be given more, and he will have an abundance. Whoever does not have, even what he has will be taken from him ..." is another way to state this principle.

"Then what is it? What's the secret? How come I can't get in sync with life? Why is it that when the world zigs I zag?" you're wondering. "What is it I need to know? What am I missing out on?" are the two questions that haunt you. Pursuing these two questions runs you ragged, in fact, and keeps you hopping around like the harried plate twirler in a circus sideshow.

"Yes, that's right; that's exactly how I feel. So what do I do now?" And this very question is the one that prompts you to keep those plates spinning. What you'll learn in *Freedom From The Ties That Bind* is something that may never have occurred to you before: you'll see the sense—and sanity—in *doing nothing*! Imagine: you'll learn to *not* respond to the call to action that's kept you running in circles up till now.

The thought in your mind now is, "What do you mean 'do nothing'?! I have *too much* to do; I'll never catch up! Besides, I'm not lazy; I'm a *doer*! If I don't do it all, who will? If I don't keep up the pace, I'll fall behind—and then where will I be?" And the answer is: you'll be off the treadmill and out of the rat race. From this new vantage point on the sidelines you'll gain a *true view* of your life and events. From this solid ground you'll reap your heart's desires.

Wise, serene, happy, prosperous people see their lives and events differently than others do. A wise man cannot be duped or mislead. A genuinely happy woman cannot be swayed by "bad news." A prosperous individual doesn't panic over an item on the evening news or a sensational newspaper headline. These peoples' wisdom, happiness, and wealth permanently reside within, not without.

What you've learned, and now believe, is that happiness, for example, is something you either win or create for yourself. To be happy, we believe we must create happy surroundings: happy children, a happy spouse, happy co-workers, and a happy home. And in the same way, we attempt to "gain wisdom" by reading deep books, lining our walls with leather-bound volumes, and joining the literary guild. We see happiness and wisdom as external "things" that must be conquered, acquired, and added to ourselves.

Now let me ask you: is a truly happy woman only happy at home or is she also happy in a crowded shopping mall? And is a wise man only wise while in his office handling his affairs, or is he also wise when visiting a carnival? The answers are obvious. Anyone who genuinely is happy or wise is that way in *every* situation. He or she brings that quality everywhere he or she goes. Wisdom and happiness are that person's *nature*. The converse is also true: An angry or ignorant person carries anger and ignorance everywhere and into all situations with him or her. And this explains the fact why "what you see is what you get." If we're angry, we see the world through angry eyes, so anger is what we experience. If we're wise, we find wisdom in what we see, and so truth is what we live.

All this makes perfect sense. Our nature determines what we receive from life. To use an analogy, what we see in the mirror can only be what we are. To change that reflection we must change ourselves. But the way we've been going about it is the equivalent of working on the reflection in the mirror. In other words, as Guy Finley explains, we've been frantically trying to become happy by attempting to apply a smile to our reflection in the mirror!

Again, all of this is perfectly logical. So where do we go wrong and why do we keep uselessly working on the reflection rather our own nature which determines the reflection? This is why *Freedom From The Ties That Bind* is such a unique book and one of only a few you'll find that cuts straight to the problem and vividly instructs how to apply the only true and lasting solution. From the first passages of Guy Finley's Special Message and his penetrating "Forty Ways To Determine Your Level of Freedom," you'll know you're finally onto something truly different and more powerful than anything you've studied before.

When you change your nature you change your world. Place a happy person and a bitter person together in the same room and they experience that room in completely different ways. So where do we begin this process of changing our nature? We begin by understanding and observing our present nature and how it operates. People do not understand themselves and are their own source of constant confusion and worry. But now, with this guide, you'll learn to *see* your anger with new eyes that also see that you no longer have to *be* that anger. You'll realize that you don't have to act on those worrisome, anxious thoughts of futility and depression; instead, you'll understand that you can calmly observe them without becoming them.

Did you notice that a part of you relaxed just now and felt relieved upon reading these words? *That's* the hidden part of your nature this special book introduces you to and encourages you to become more and more acquainted with. You will experience an actual change in your very nature. As you do, your reflection in the mirror will begin to change! *This* is the change you've sought all this time; *this* is the call you've responded to but not yet answered.

Freedom From The Ties That Bind is different from most every other book, technique, or discipline you've ever attempted because it introduces and addresses the one key principle that is the least understood: you are not your thoughts. You do not create your thoughts, and you do not have to obey any thought. Being a receiver of thought, just as with a radio, you have the power to turn the dial! This is a marvelously freeing, uplifting, and powerful fact, and the more you learn the more your own life will become what you've always desired.

I sought the door to these principles for many years and finally discovered it in my late thirties when I heard Guy Finley on a national radio talk show. No one had ever described me so accurately. He understood me better than I did—my hopes, my fears, my attempts and failures. He had already traversed the shaky ground I was wearily trying to cross.

I sought him out and began attending his lectures. The smile on my face grew larger with each one. I finally began to understand what had baffled me: money, children, marriage ... life! I learned that there isn't a separate set of rules for each niche of our lives; rather, there's one enveloping principle that, when understood, explains it all to us. When *this* new understanding becomes our focus, and not individual goals and events, everything begins to clear up.

If you've ever felt that life was a great train station and you've been a confused but aspiring passenger, you can relax now: you've reached the boarding platform to higher places ...

Welcome aboard!

Ken Roberts
Grants Pass, Oregon

Ken Roberts is founder and president of The Ken Roberts Companies, a multinational corporation recognized the world over for its financial education programs.

A Special Message
From The Author

THINK FOR A MOMENT WHAT YOUR LIFE WOULD BE LIKE IF you lived in a world where reality and your happiness were one and the same—where everything that happened in your life was always just what you wanted. Imagine it!

No event, no condition could do anything but contribute to your well-being. Every day, everyone and everything would work in your favor. And since your contentment in this new world arises from the procession of its natural events, your greatest pleasure would be to just let go, and let life flow by as it pleases.

Could there be such a world where contentment isn't just the momentary absence of conflict? Is there really a peaceful place where love and happiness aren't just the flip side of a constantly spinning coin? Let me assure you, there is. And we're much closer to this higher world than first thoughts might allow. In fact, this realm where wholeness rules is right within each of us. But perhaps you already sense the truth of this. Most do. At one level or another all of us know that our lives are incomplete; that our real Home is yet to be found.

But sensing there's a higher world and standing within it are vastly different. What we don't understand is how to reach the door to this kingdom, *open it, and walk in*. Too bold? Not at all! Only to our own conditioned and captive consciousness does the idea of full freedom sound impossible. Its unspoken, but pervasive, attitude toward life is to find ways to make the best of a bad situation; to not rock the boat at any cost. And so, almost without a question, we've all paid the price. But no longer.

Settling for anything less than complete self liberation is like agreeing to spend your life on a well-appointed slave ship—where rowing duties are only every other week! Stop thinking in terms of finding ways to improve any life that includes feelings of compulsory servitude. Begin the process of becoming fully conscious of *another kind of Life* altogether. *That's* what *Freedom From The Ties That Bind* is all about!

LET WHAT YOU LIKE LEAD YOU ALL THE WAY TO SELF LIBERATION

Do you like to be pleasantly surprised? Who doesn't! So allow me to give you some good news: as you read through this book, you're going to find dozens of helpful ideas and techniques that will both surprise and delight you. In fact, let me introduce you to one of them right now. This amazing new principle is guaranteed to help you extract the inner riches from each of the pages that follow.

It may happen as you read through this new material that some of its higher lessons will seem confusing at first. If that happens, you can still proceed successfully. Here's how. *Just let what you like lead you from one step to the next.* Let me show you how this unusual rule of thumb can work in your favor, and how it can lead you to a life that is fully fearless and free. Please consider the following.

When we listen to the moving compositions of a Bach or a Beethoven, we simply sit back, relax, and enjoy the music. We don't have to understand the complex harmonies flowing around and through us to appreciate them. Why? Because within each of us there exists a part of our own secret nature that, because it's already in a state of Harmony, knows when it hears something right.

In a similar fashion, Higher Ideas, like their musical counterpart of beautiful chords, also have a certain "sound." They either ring true to us, or not.

Can you see the beauty in learning to rely on this internal process? Whether we like something or not is very simple; clear cut. What we appreciate takes no thought. So, if we find we're attracted to a new idea, if somehow it resonates within us—even though it may challenge formerly treasured beliefs—our *interest* follows without effort. And from our own newly heightened interest comes a willingness to use that new idea—to work with it—to examine those beliefs we formally held as true. Before long, in this freshly tilled ground of our own inner life, insights begin to flower. There's new life. Its vital presence fuels our wish to continue with our inner studies. And as each new self discovery takes us still deeper, still higher, it dawns on us there's no end to this beautiful process.

The story of these unfolding inner stages reveals that we can indeed appreciate—and grow from—something we don't initially understand. As we learn to trust this new and higher form of our intuition, we also learn that our appreciation of each truthful idea is somehow connected to the essence of that same truth. And as each truth comes to us in this fashion, *so does its strength and its freedom become ours.* We've earned our first glimpse of a truly free mind.

One more important word before we begin our journey together: letting what you like lead you through this book doesn't mean you won't feel some resistance to the principles and insights about to be revealed. This inner opposition usually occurs each time the habitual mind can't find a place to put what is new within the framework of its own pre-existing structure. Should you find yourself caught up in this internal struggle, remember the following truth: its wisdom is both the instruction and the encouragement you need to choose in favor of yourself. *For true inner growth to take place, former mental concepts must be fully replaced, so be willing to let go of what you think you know.* You'll discover that as you allow this healthy exchange to take place, a natural healing of the mind and heart follows without any effort.

There really is a way to be free.

Like most men and women today, your life probably belongs to everyone and everything else but you. But you can win it back! You can choose to live the way you want. Think of it!

Even the most difficult people won't be able to turn your head or test your temper. Your relationships will be founded on choice, not in compromise. What other freedoms can you expect? For a pleasant surprise just imagine:

1. Letting go of that terrible need that's always made you feel as though you have to prove yourself to everyone you meet.

2. Seeing all anxious and nagging doubts about your future disappear.

3. Knowing that you never again have to look at your own life through the eyes of any past defeat.

And there's more: you'll no longer find it necessary to try and please that cruel, inner task master who's forever telling you that you're just not good enough. Here's why. Once you've realized the great secret of spiritual liberation, more than a million tomorrows can come and go, but you'll know that none of them can give you any more than *you already are right now. This realization is full and final freedom from the ties that bind.*

Your inner success is guaranteed. Just dare to place yourself on the side of yourself that appreciates what is true *just because it's true.* Let what you like lead you all the way to self liberation. You will be free.

CHAPTER 1

Discover The Freedom You Need To Live The Way You Want

I N OUR QUEST TO WIN FREEDOM FROM THE TIES THAT BIND, we spend most of our lives struggling to overcome vague foes that fade in and out, like the shadows that move across the forest floor each time the sun moves behind a cloud.

Yet, for all of these battles engaged and won, for all the changes we've made in our lifestyles and relationships, one thing remains basically the same. We still feel tied down! There's a stone in our soul we can't shake loose.

And that's why, even though everything else about how to liberate ourselves may remain vague, the following realization cuts through this psychic fog like the bright beam of a lighthouse on a stormy night: any real change in the world of our *outer life* is going to have to originate from a change in our *inner life*. Still more to the point: *blaming any exterior condition in our lives as the culprit behind our feeling tied down or captive is like getting angry at our shoes for being laced too tight!*

If we're ever to satisfy our longing to live the way we want, if we're ever to be fully independent and free, we must let the facts speak for themselves: regardless of the way things may appear on the surface, the ties that bind us have their roots hidden in our minds. We are lashed down with our own thoughts. They wrap themselves around our hearts and make our spirit suffer. And that's why our battle for freedom must be waged within, for that's where the ground is that must be recaptured.

Even the gripping fear of failing finances, or painful worry over the aging of the body, has its beginnings in the invisible interior of a person—in that individual's thoughts and feelings—and more specifically still, in the level of understanding from which those thoughts and feelings arise. All freedoms, as well as the heavy spirit we bear in their absence, are a question of consciousness. This is why freedom from the ties that bind must begin with a change in our being.

So now we know: the good struggle which we must take up isn't with person, place, or circumstance, but with our present level of consciousness—a level of mind that is itself a captive of its own unsuspected enslaved condition. Johann von Goethe, the highly celebrated German poet and philosopher, spoke to the importance of this fact and its relevance to real self rescue when he said, "None are more hopelessly enslaved than those who falsely believe they are free."

Goethe's wise counsel also hints to us that each bit of light we can direct into this darkness known as self deception is really the same as the seed of self liberation. So welcome the light by gladly volunteering for the upcoming inner exercise.

FORTY WAYS TO DETERMINE YOUR LEVEL OF INNER FREEDOM

Want to know how free you really are? Good! You're about to be presented with a unique opportunity to learn all about your individual level of inner liberty.

Assembled here for your self study is a very special kind of test. But don't worry! You can't fail this examination. This test is unlike any you've ever taken before. It's designed to help you gaze into yourself and then use what you see there as a gauge to help you determine your level of freedom. Here's how it works.

Following are forty simple internal indicators for evaluating just how far along you actually are on freedom's path. As you review each of the inner liberties on the list, just note mentally to yourself whether or not that particular freedom belongs to you. If you have to think about whether you're free in one way or another, you're probably not as free in that area as you'd give yourself to believe. Relax. This is to be expected. Which means let's not forget our aim in this evaluation. Our intention is simply to learn what's true about ourselves, *not to prove anything to ourselves*.

You may find some of the upcoming list surprising. If that happens, let it. And then feel free to consider you never knew such a freedom could exist for you because, up until now, you were sure you had no choice but to live restrained in this area. Now you know better! Allow these forty freedoms to awaken and stir that secret part of you that knows living in any kind of bondage is a lie. Then follow your own natural sensing all the way to the free life.

You're Well Along Freedom's Path When:

1. You have no desire to change places in life with anyone else.

2. You step over setbacks without stopping or looking back.

3. You don't think about your sex life.

4. You accept and appreciate praise, but never take it to heart.

5. You don't overeat or feel driven to diet.

6. You meet and do what's true without fear of the consequences.

7. You really don't want anything from anyone.

8. You stop thinking about how much money you may or may not have.

9. You don't carry any upset from the last moment into the present one.

10. You have no interest in old resentments.

11. You start spending more time alone and enjoying it more.

12. You stop dreaming of the perfect vacation.

13. You lose all interest in trying to win mental arguments.

14. You're neither frightened nor shocked by the evening news.

15. You stop making deals with yourself.

16. You dress for comfort, not for compliments.

17. You don't blame anyone else for the way you feel.

18. You forget what it was you didn't like about someone.

19. You're awake to and spontaneously considerate of the needs of others.

20. You see beauty in life where you never could see it before.

21. Your life gets progressively simpler.

22. You see where you're wrong sooner than later, and stop defending yourself faster.

23. You do what you don't want to do, and you do it with a lighter spirit.

24. You're not afraid of having nothing to say or do, if that's your true condition.

25. You can take criticism without cringing away from the truth that it may hold.

26. You have no concern for what others may think of you.

27. You stop trying to make others see life in your way.

28. You enjoy the sound of silence as much or more than the sound of your own voice.

29. You see the same unpleasant traits within yourself that have made you shun others.

30. You say what you want, and not what you think others may want to hear you say.

31. You actually enjoy hearing about the good fortune of someone else.

32. You see more and more just how unfree you and others really are.

33. Your moods are fewer, lighter, and move on much quicker.

34. You see society is destroying itself and that the only solution is in self change.

35. You can listen to others without the need to tell them what you know.

36. You don't find a thrill in any kind of fear.

37. You know that forgiveness of others is the kindest thing you can do for yourself.

38. You realize the world is the way it is because you are the way you are.

39. You'd rather *not* think about yourself.

40. You can't come up with one good reason why you should ever be anxious or frightened.

There's one more important point to bring to our attention before we continue with our self studies: *never discourage over your present location!*

Discouragement is a negative emotion with more than one trick up its dark sleeve. It tricks you into mentally or emotionally dwelling in the very place you want to leave. Drop all such sorrow permanently by daring to see through this deception of the unconscious mind.

The very fact that you know there's farther to go before your journey to freedom is complete also tells you that wherever you may find yourself standing today—or a thousand days from now—is just a place you have to pass through on your way to where you're going. And you're going to be free! So agree to put all discouraging places where they belong: behind you!

Who you really are, your True Nature, is no more tied to the kind of places or person *you've been* than the wind is tied to the skies through which it moves. Your past, who and what you once were, is just that: *the past*, a place within your psyche with no more reality to it than the picture of a castle on a postcard is made from stone.

As you're about to discover, through the hundreds of encouraging and healing insights revealed in this book, you have a Destination far beyond where *you find yourself standing today*.

To help speed your inner progress, and for additional benefits from this chapter, go back over the entire list of freedoms at least one more time. In your second review of these forty points of freedom, notice which ones are most attractive to you. Mark down their corresponding numbers on a sheet of paper.

For instance, as #27 points out, maybe you're weary of being caught in that familiar losing battle of trying to make friends and family see life through *your* all-knowing eyes. It took a long time, but you're beginning to see just how blind you've been. Now you want to be free of your own inconsiderate and impatient egotism. But try as you may, something within won't let you let go of your unconscious certainty that you know better than anyone else. Good! You may not know it yet, but you're drawing near a very special spiritual victory.

Or perhaps like #10 on the list suggests, maybe you sense how self destructive it is to resent someone else. And you're tired of being a slave to refueling your own burning mind. You want to be free of those internal, infernal fires. Again, that's good. Now you know two important things.

1. You're not as free as you would like to be.

2. Something is interfering with your wish to be free.

It may not seem so at first, but your new findings are a great start. Now keep going. Use this list and your discoveries to help you ignite your wish to be free. Then step back and welcome the spiritual firestorm. Watch as it burns away the ties that bind. This is what it means to let the Light fight for you.

Two Amazing Stories About Self Imprisonment

One of the most fascinating nature programs I ever watched on TV chronicled the events surrounding the capture and training of wild elephants. These huge, kindly creatures are extremely intelligent; their strength and endurance, legendary. And yet, for all their might and innate wisdom, those beasts which are captured are soon pressed into man's service and rarely stray in duty or discipline. But by far the most intriguing aspect of the documentary was the unspoken spiritual lesson it revealed in showing the last few stages of the elephants submission to captivity. Here was a great truth hidden in plain sight for those who could see it.

As these powerful, ten thousand-pound animals neared the end of their indoctrination, they were held prisoners not by steel cages or high-tensile cables, but by a small fiber cord tied around one of their ankles! Any motivated human adult would have the strength to break this size cord. What was it that kept these highly intelligent elephants from just snapping these strands and escaping to freedom? One of the trainers explained this amazing phenomenon.

In the early stages of intensive training, the legs of the wild elephants are shackled and cross-tied with huge ropes impossible for them to break. For days on end the massive beasts struggle to free themselves, but always to no avail. The hope of liberating themselves through their own strength eventually fades and, shortly after, a great weariness comes over each creature.

As the great beasts become slowly resigned to their restricted freedom, the trainers gradually replace their thick leg ties with thinner and smaller ones. And, before too long, having been fully conditioned to the impossibility of ever breaking free from its ties, all that restrains the largest land creature living today is a cord no thicker your finger. The elephants remain as willing, but unwitting captives of their own inability to understand their true condition: they could break their binds with just one small tug. And yet, they can't see past the certainty of their own captivity.

If the spiritual lesson in this illustration isn't clear yet, the following one will remove all doubts.

In his classic book, *Meetings with Remarkable Men*, George Gurdjieff tells all about his own worldwide search for freedom from the ties that bind. He made the following incredible discovery during his travels, and its lesson proved pivotal in eventually achieving his own liberation.

One afternoon, high in a remote region of some Asian mountain, he happened upon a small group of villagers taunting a young man who was being held captive in a most extraordinary way. Gurdjieff couldn't believe his eyes.

The only thing keeping the unfortunate man a prisoner and unable to flee the abusive villagers was a circle drawn in the dirt around his feet! Nothing real was holding him. That is to say, nothing real except his very real beliefs in the religious doctrines of his tribe.

Gurdjieff learned that the young man came from a small, extremely orthodox group of mountain people; and it was their spiritual customs that accounted for the behavior he had witnessed. Their ancient traditions held and taught that if or when any one of them should ever come to stand within a circle, that to break it themselves, by stepping outside of that circle's lines, would bring a terrible curse, or even death.

The young man Gurdjieff watched in amazement that day was unable to escape his captors because he was a captive of his own mental framework.

These two stories hold important lessons for us. Both provide a provocative glimpse into the possibility of winning freedom for ourselves, as each true story suggests something unsuspected about the real nature of the ties that hold us down.

Our continuing studies will give us the tools we need to transform this first glimpse into the triumph of self liberation.

THIS INSIGHT LEADS TO FREEDOM FROM SELF CREATED CAPTIVITY

I once asked a small gathering of students to identify what they thought was keeping them from being quietly free and happy human beings. I knew the success of the lesson intended for that meeting would be measurably heightened if all of us could arrive at some consensus about the nature of what keeps us feeling like captives. And from the comments that came pouring out, one thing was clear. Everyone in attendance felt tied down by one thing or another.

But, before we get to the very important object of that night's lesson, let's look at some of the students' observations that helped to set it up.

John G. said he felt tied down by his past. Regrets over personal losses from disappointing ventures and his own dashed hopes from failed relationships were some of the feelings he told us he just couldn't shake.

And, as these things happen, his comment stirred Lynn M., who added to John's list saying she felt haunted by some great opportunity that she'd missed, as well as by some bad mistakes in her distant past that bothered her still.

When Paul P. spoke, he was troubled by having once said something very cruel to a loved one that he now wished he could somehow take back. And that made Bob C. speak up. The heavy weight he carried was something important that he never had the courage to say to some significant other, and now it was too late.

Larry G. then said he wasn't free because of his constant craving for approval and attention, which made his wife, Clara, admit she was tired of always harshly judging people, including herself.

Other reasons why the students felt like they were captives had to do with hunger for recognition, the compulsion to accumulate wealth, seeking power over people and events, and the search for physical perfection. And when I asked, most admitted to feeling haunted by recurring resentment towards someone who either once had or who currently was dominating them. The atmosphere was emotional, but very honest. The stage had been well set for the special lesson which was given as follows.

Nothing real holds us down, or back, or from being completely free. We are not trapped in any relationship, professional or personal, past or present. Nor is any lost opportunity the reason why we still feel confused about our direction in life today. Nothing we've ever done, or failed to do, limits the possibility of our knowing complete self liberty in this very moment. The truth is: we are free right now.

"I've heard this idea before, and while it's certainly a beautiful sentiment, it frustrates me every time I hear it! How can you say that nothing real is keeping me from being free when, almost every day, in one way or another, my life feels like a hundred restrictions have been placed upon it: when to stop, when to go; don't go there, better get there quick; smile at him, not at her; speak up for this, shut up about that! At times I feel like one of those wild horses that has ropes around its neck, all pulling from different directions at the same time!"

Please listen carefully. It is not the experiences of life, in themselves, that tell you full freedom isn't possible. It's what you're telling yourself about those experiences that has you certain your captivity is reality. But nothing real has a hold on you. A short true story right out of my own backyard will help illustrate how we are kept captives of our own undeveloped consciousness.

AN IMPORTANT LIFE LESSON ABOUT
SELF LIBERATION FROM A BIRD IN A BLOCK

One morning, just before sunrise, I was up and sitting in my favorite chair waiting for my favorite part of each morning: the coming of the birds.

My outdoor patio, besides housing my bonsai trees, is a haven for little feathered creatures. Of course their affection for the location probably doesn't have anything to do with the fact that I set out lots of seed for them!

The small finches, juncos, and sparrows love to hop in and out of my collection of diminutive trees which sit on makeshift shelves of old timbers supported by cinder blocks. It's great fun to watch their aerobatics as each little band of birds flies in and competes for the seed I've thrown on top of the boards and blocks.

This particular morning though something amazing took place just as the sun made its appearance. As usual, the patio area was a beehive of bird activity. I was watching one bright male finch who was having a great time fleeting in and out of the cinder blocks' open cells. Chirping and fighting off various intruders, he was as busy as a bird could be. And then something strange happened. The flitting finch suddenly came to a dead stop. He just froze right where he stood in the center of one of the bottom cinder block's open cells.

I quickly checked all of the other birds' behavior, as I knew that sometimes when a predator is around a bird will try the freeze-tactic for self protection. But not one of the other birds was acting nervous or worried. What had happened to this one frozen finch? There was no visible explanation for his strange behavior.

A full five minutes later, I began to worry that maybe something was organically wrong with this little stiff bird. Even when his band of friends finally took off for parts unknown, he remained motionless, glued right where he was. I was completely baffled. And then I saw it! There was an explanation after all! But it was almost too much to believe.

My earlier suspicion proved to be the right one. The little finch was actually transfixed in fear. But the source of his paralyzing fear was nothing other than his own shadow! As unbelievable as it sounds, here's what had happened.

Just at the moment when the finch had hopped into the opening of that one cinder block cell, the sun had reached enough of a zenith to create tall morning shadows. And at that very moment, dark shapes—*including his*—were cast onto the concrete floor through the window of the cinder block cell. Only the finch didn't know that what he perceived as an unknown silent stalker *was really just his own elongated shadow!*

The happy ending to this strange story of the bird in the block came a minute or two later, when the sun had then moved high enough in the sky to make the morning shadows vanish from the patio floor. As if by magic, the finch was released from his spell. Off he flew, chirping out his hard fought victory over the menacing figure he had faced and fooled.

In scale, meaning in much the same way only at a different level, this true story of the bird in the block tells the tale of the ties that bind our life too. For just as our feathered friend was held temporary prisoner by a phantom shape with no substance, we too have long been captives of nothing; nothing, that is to say, other than the shadows of *our own thoughts*. How is this possible? The following factual insight gives us the understanding we need to begin freeing ourselves.

A New Inner Understanding To Put You In Charge Of All Outer Circumstances

Barring those moments when we find ourselves in real physical danger, *conditions, of themselves, have absolutely no authority over us*. It's true. No event or circumstance has any power to make us feel one way or another. The only command any condition may have over us is that which we unconsciously surrender to it. And what we've given away, we can take back. Insight coupled with action is all the power we need. Here's why.

All conditions, events, and circumstances are neutral—they are neither for you, nor against you.

Spinoza, the great Dutch philosopher and metaphysician, tried to help his students grasp this meaningful idea. He taught, "All things which occasioned me any anxiety or worry had in themselves nothing of good or evil, except as in so far as the mind was moved by them."

You're invited to prove this important concept for yourself by taking a special inner adventure in the form of the following exercise. The new freedoms that come with your discoveries will belong to you. This exercise is great fun too!

The next time you're with a group of people, friends or family, or even out at a mall or restaurant, *be an event watcher!*

What's an event watcher? We'll learn more about this unique practice in a later chapter of this book, but for now, an event watcher is:

1. Someone who better wants to understand that events are always neutral in their origin.

2. Someone who sits quietly at a psychological distance from events as they unfold.

3. Someone who watches to see how events make others behave, and who is self observing as well.

4. Someone who doesn't confuse his or her reaction to any given event for the event itself.

For our lesson I've produced a simplified example of how this profitable inner life exercise might be practiced. But remember, making your own discoveries is vital for your development, so learn to watch events wherever you are, all the time.

Let's say you're out with a group of friends for a meal at a nice restaurant. Everything is casual, relaxed—just as it should be, a pleasantly neutral atmosphere. And then, someone at your table says, "Did you hear the news! They just announced that the price of coffee is going to go through the ceiling!"

In the next instant, because of that one comment, the atmosphere at your table suddenly shifts. You can feel it, and your awareness calls you into a wide awake state. You know it's time to be an event watcher.

So you relax, sit back, and begin watching everything around you as it begins to unfold. This one point is clear from the start: the fact that coffee beans just jumped into a higher price range is truly a neutral event.

As you watch the effect of the news ripple over your friends, you can see that most of them have little or no reaction at all. Why? Various reasons: the most likely of which is that they don't drink much coffee!

If you continue to watch the event unfold, the odds are you'll soon observe one man or woman in your group become a captive of the news. But don't judge, just watch. *All judgements of others as they're drawn into an event make you both a part and a prisoner of that same event.* So stay awake to this tendency. Stay free.

As an event watcher how do you know when someone has fallen victim to conditions and become a psychic prisoner?

He or she will make some comment that the way the world turns just isn't fair, especially as it revolves around his or her interests; or you'll be able to see his or her spirits sink before your eyes. But remain detached. As long as you don't jump into it, the negative atmosphere of anyone else that may be around you is just another neutral event, *as far as you're concerned!* This higher spiritual standpoint allows you to remain watchful and ask the next two important questions of yourself.

If conditions are really powerless to make you, or any other individual, a captive, then what's happened to your companion in this illustration? What is it that has captured him or her?

While any imprisoned person can come up with as many reasons as there are stars to justify a sudden surge of negativity, the invisible cause of his or her captivity is always the same. So, let's just say for this example that the person thrown into the invisible prison over the rumor of increased coffee costs is probably the one in your party who tends to consume it the most, while possibly being the least able to afford its rise in price. But let's not lose sight of the exercise!

Was it *the event* which tied that individual up in knots? Did *the conditions* of supply and demand as they concerned the economics of coffee produce that person's prison? Or was his or her temporary confinement created only by an unseen thought as it whispered to him or her in undetectable tones, "Oh no! What's going to happen *to me* if I can no longer afford to enjoy my morning coffee?"

The lesson from your first excellent adventure as an event watcher should be clear: *it's never the event or the condition that holds us captive, but the way we think toward it that creates our sense of captivity.*

The immense implications of our discovery hold more than just the promise of finding freedom from the ties that bind. In Chapter 2 we'll realize the existence of another kind of mind altogether: a *Free Mind* that never gets tangled up in a mental web because its nature doesn't dwell in the realm of thought.

TEN KEYS FOR GAINING GREATER SELF LIBERATION

Help yourself to the keys of self liberation hidden in these next ten insights. In this summary section of Chapter 1, as well in each similar section in the remaining chapters, take the time you need to let each concentrated idea sink into your heart and mind.

The truths you are about to meet are actually alive. If you embrace their healing presence, their life becomes yours. This is a hint of what it means to know the Truth, and to then be set free by that Truth.

1. Nothing in this world—or any other—can stop you from finding, and then knowing, freedom from the ties that bind.

2. When it comes to changing the unhappy conditions you meet in life, remember that nothing about your life can change ... until *you* do.

3. Give yourself permission to long for a freedom so great that it includes the end of all painful longings.

4. Whatever it may be that holds you captive is nothing compared to what wants to set you free.

5. Freedom from the ties that bind begins with getting completely fed up with being all tied up.

6. In any inwardly restrictive moment of anger, worry, or fear, always remember there's nothing outside of *you* tightening the ropes.

7. A hundred times a day, notice how unfree you feel, and then feel free to drop that feeling.

8. Nothing real has a hold on you, so become highly suspicious of those parts of yourself that are certain you must live with limitations.

9. The next time you feel overwhelmed by some contrary condition, remember the only power that circumstance has over you *is what you want from it*.

10. Your experience of this world is determined by how you think toward it, which is why, as you change the way you think toward yourself, you also change the world you live in.

CHAPTER 2

Break Through To A New And Secret "You" That's Already Free

IN OUR EARLIER STUDIES FROM THE FIRST CHAPTER, WE learned how wild elephants behave as captive as if wrapped up in steel cables, even though all that really holds them is a single thin cord.

Of course, it's easy to reason that these awesome beasts have been conditioned by their trainers. After all, their minds have been bent to a superior will. Animals can't think as we do. They have no choice. They remain enslaved because they are first captured by something wiser than themselves.

And yet, what about the young man Gurdjieff observed who was a prisoner of only a circle drawn in the dirt? Why couldn't he escape? Was he, like the wild elephants, a captive of something more wise than himself? Was he too a victim of superior forces acting upon him from without?

No, it's quite clear. The man in the circle was a prisoner of *interior forces* with the power to lock up his exterior life. Simply stated, he was tied up by a system of unquestioned religious beliefs. And his inescapable prison of the moment was nothing other than bars fabricated from the mental stuff of his very own thoughts.

Our insight into the irony of this young captive's strange situation is really a ray of light from the Great Secret Of Self Liberation. For in the light of our discovery we see not only a glimpse of the real cause behind our own captive condition, but our studies also beg us to ask the following important question:

How is it possible for a man or woman to be both *prisoner* and, without ever knowing it, his or her own *prison maker* at the same time?

"Yes! That's exactly what I want to know! If we are the thinker—as is our unquestioned belief—the creator of this tool we call thought—then how can these same thoughts hold us captive? Such a condition, if it exists, is like a man being held prisoner by a hammer he holds in his own hand! It just doesn't make any sense. Either we're in control of our own thoughts and feelings or we're not! Something just isn't adding up here, but I'm not sure what it is or, what to make of it."

Anxiety or confusion over our inner condition is usually a sign we're nearer the truth of something about ourselves than we're ready to admit. Our primary fear here is in not knowing what will happen to us if we open our eyes all the way and consciously acknowledge what we see. Yet, if we're to succeed in our quest for freedom, we must dare to make our invisible lives as clearly visible to ourselves as we can. So, which is it? Are we in charge of our own thoughts and feelings, or are we really their secret captives?

"It seems to me that I'm capable of starting my own thought process rolling. But, on the other hand, there are also those times when I'm powerless to stop the cascading momentum of those same thoughts. For instance, I may begin thinking about one of my past pleasant experiences and, before I realize what's happening, I'll be taken over by some sad memory I never intended to consider. Or maybe I'll be planning how to better secure my future and the next thing I know I'm an anxious wreck for fear I won't be able to succeed with my plans! And when I'm shackled by these sorry or stressed out feelings, there's nothing I can do to get them off of my back. Thank goodness they eventually fade away; or something nice happens to me and their unpleasant presence is replaced with a brighter one.

"But, clearly, this isn't the same as being in charge of my own inner life. And isn't that what you wanted to know? So, even though this is hard to admit, I don't know how to arrive at any other conclusion. But, what does it all mean? What's the value in discovering that I can be turned into a prisoner of my own thoughts?"

More than you can possibly imagine right now. But, for one thing, it means you're beginning to wake up just a little bit.

"Wake up? Wake up to what?"

The illusion that you're the thinker.

"What do you mean? If I'm not the thinker of my own thoughts then who, or what, is? It certainly feels to me like I'm the one doing the thinking."

Yes, and for good reason too. Whether in our waking life, or in the dreams that visit our evening's rest, thoughts and feelings fill our every present moment. But just because you can feel or sense all of their diverse characteristics—such as worry, fear, fantasy, impatience, relief, courage, or compulsiveness—doesn't make *the "you"* that experiences these movements *real*; anymore than standing under the cascade of a waterfall, and feeling its flow, means that your nature is water.

Thoughts and feelings are energies. They're forces that we have passing through us continually. And each has a distinct nature. But neither any one, nor all of these mental or emotional qualities put together, *is who we really are.*

Again, we feel the heat of the sun on our face, but we know better than to think that we're a blaze. And yet when we feel the fire of an angry thought or emotion, we believe we are that burning sensation. *We are not!* We only make the mistake of thinking that we are; which is why these painful and unwanted internal fires go on and on, but never out.

"This is unbelievable. And yet it all makes perfect sense. Please continue. What else do I need to understand to cut myself loose from these invisible psychic strings?"

DISCOVER THE LARGER LIFE BEYOND THE FALSE SELF

First, let's slow down a little. We must be clear. It is *not* our thoughts and feelings that have us tied up, or that keep us running after rainbows.

"I thought you said it's all in the way we think that's at the core of our being psychic captives?"

Yes, but that's not the chief problem. Which is why the control of our thoughts, or finding various ways to deal with troublesome emotions, never brings the freedom promised with such disciplines.

"Then what is the real difficulty?"

We live from a false nature, a false sense of self. And yet, the imitation life of this unconscious nature is so complete, most men and women never suspect their lives are being lived out for them by something with less substance than a shadow.

"But how could such a condition come to be without anyone knowing it?"

Like the invisible winds that move the branches on the trees, we live in a world of an unseen, but ceaseless, flood of thoughts and feelings. In some sense, we're constantly being washed over by the waves of all past human experience. These ancient forces, combined with our individual mechanical associative reactions to present events, all serve to give each of us the sense of a self with both a past and a future.

But *this self is fictitious*. Its nature is a kind of ghost house, a complex but empty structure created by the stream of thoughts and feelings that provide it with its false sense of life. Throughout this book, we'll refer to this aspect of our own unconscious, undeveloped nature as the *me mind*.

English author and scholar D.L. Pendlebury says of this false nature: "(This) self is an entirely illusory entity, constantly changing, full of contradictions which only habit prevents us from discerning. But above all the self is—selfish. As if flying in panic from any recognition of its own nothingness, it feverishly erects edifices of self importance, self aggrandizement, self love. More binding than any prison, since we unthinkingly take its very walls for reality, it prevents us from ever realizing the true significance of our being here."

We can now summarize the central point of this part of our study as follows: the me mind, the false self, has no control over the thoughts and feelings that tie it down, because *its only life is derived from their constant movement*.

If this lower mind could be made conscious of its own actual deceived condition, we'd be released from the psychic grip it has upon us. That's why *our* task is to become increasingly aware of ourselves. Inner light is the only power that can resolve the captivity created by the inner darkness. More insight into the life-cycle of this false nature will make things clearer.

Imagine a man who has come to truly believe that pizza is the key to global peace. His false ideas about the well-being of the planet create his multiple false needs. For instance, he sincerely feels, in order for peace to prevail, there must be pizza shops on every corner of every block in each city throughout the entire world. So, his false needs, based on a half-baked idea about pizza and global harmony being tied together, create his false desires. And these false desires give rise to false fears— fears which *feel real*, but have no real foundation.

This man can't sleep at nights thinking about what happens if the world runs out of pizza dough. Or what if someone corners the market on pizza sauce or pepperoni! He suffers over all the possibilities of a pizza-less world that will never know peace! And so his sufferings create his new and equally false needs all over again. The cycle of self deception is complete. And then it starts all over again. This is the life of the false self.

Now let's consciously switch the pizza in our illustration for an image not so obviously silly. Take any one of the values prized by our society. You fill in the blanks; but don't forget the desire for money, approval, power, constant company, fame, esteem, authority, or possessions. Do this exercise in earnest and you'll see why there's no end to why we feel tied down.

"But why don't we see this? The way you've explained it, so many things which never made sense before, make sense at last. For instance, I've always wondered what was the real cause of greed. Now I think I understand. The only life the false self can have is to want more and more since there's nothing real that can ever satisfy its false desires. But where have we been? Why can't we see what's right before our very eyes?"

This is an excellent question! Let's allow the brilliant English philosopher and essayist William Law to answer it for us: "The greatest part of mankind ... may be said to be asleep, and that particular way of life which takes up each man's mind, thoughts and actions, may be very well called his particular dream. This degree of vanity is equally visible in every form and order of life. The learned and the ignorant, the rich and the poor, are all in the same state of slumber."

"I've heard this idea before, that human beings live in a state of spiritual sleep. But what does it mean to be asleep to myself? And if the life I've always known isn't my Real Life, then what is? What would I awaken to find that I don't have now?"

Your True Nature.

To more fully appreciate the broader implications of awakening to the real life of our True Nature the words of John Caird, the Scottish philosopher and Christian divine, sound out an appealing invitation: "There is provided an escape from the narrowness and poverty of the individual life, and the possibility of a life which is other and larger than our own, yet which is most truly our own. For, to be ourselves, we must be more than ourselves. What we call love is, in truth ... the losing of our individual selves to gain a larger self."

Follow Your Longing To Be Limitless All the Way To The Free Mind

The deep dissatisfaction we often feel with the littleness of our lives is not the proof our true needs for an encompassing, more complete life, can't be met. *We're intended, here and now, to know the higher pleasures that move freely through the inwardly liberated heart— including love, strength, purpose, and compassion.* The sole purpose of this book is to help you confirm this healing fact for yourself.

The following insight, along with its detailed explanation, will help you see that you're meant to know the lasting happiness your heart has been longing for: *all real needs are connected to an invisible condition that gives rise to that need.* Now, let's state this same idea in a different way: you can't have a need to be free and happy *without there being a source of freedom and happiness already in place to fill that need!* We can better understand this important idea as we look at how the rose needs sunlight to bloom.

The newly opened rose, with its sweetly perfumed petals, is actually *an expression* of the warmth and light it must receive in order to bloom. It's impossible to isolate the rose from the sun's radiance and expect the same fragrance.

The rose and all creatures great and small couldn't have the real needs they do without something being there, *already in place*, to answer *and fulfill those needs.* Let's look at a few other physical examples of how *need proves the existence of the needed.*

The porpoise and the dolphin long for the clear, deep seas. Their almost fathomless need to swim without restriction is actually a part of the very oceans they need to roam. There is no real substitute for their need.

The eagle and the hawk long for the wide-open skies. Both need to soar in order to *be* what they are. We can't separate their need from their nature anymore than we can separate their nature from the heavens they must have to express that winged-nature within. *It's all one thing.*

What do these discoveries teach us? Everything!

Our unspoken longing for full self liberation reaches down to us from a Higher World where these elevated conditions *already* exist.

Our need for freedom from the ties that bind is more than just a possibility: it's a spiritual promise waiting to be fulfilled. But there's more yet to this amazing discovery. The location of this secret world with all its bright promise resides right *within you*. And whether you choose to name this peaceable inner domain, or leave it nameless, doesn't alter the fact of its existence; or that its freedom is meant to be yours.

Throughout the recorded history of those who have sought their own Celestial Origin, this Supreme Nature has been called upon in thousands of sacred names. More recent, better-known designations include: Supermind, Overself, Christ Consciousness, Buddha Nature, Goddess Nature, Allah, Mother Divine, True Self, and Cosmic Awareness.

And while, like love itself, this Original Being can't be described, men and women, down through the ages, have found their way into its Heart; and in doing so, have also found their lives suddenly transformed and freed by its powers. For the purposes of our studies together in this book, we're going to refer to this Sovereign Self as the *Free Mind*.

The great poet and sage Ralph Waldo Emerson awakened one day to this timeless True Nature within himself. He spent the rest of his days exploring and delighting in the quiet beauty and permanent freedom he found there. His writings hint of a Heaven meant for all: "There is one mind common to all individual men. Every man is an inlet to the same and to all of the same. He that is once admitted to the right of reason is made a freeman of the whole estate. What Plato has thought, he may think; what a saint has felt, he may feel; what at any time has befallen any man, he can understand. Who hath access to this universal mind is a party to all that is or that can be, for this is the only and sovereign agent."

THERE ARE NO SUBSTITUTES FOR SELF LIBERATION

Call this new, True Nature what you will, one fact will remain unchanged: until this one, great need is met—to live from the Free Mind—no other real need of ours can be wholly satisfied. Without this fearless Foundation as our support, everything else we may fashion from the substance of our lives eventually withers and passes. Let's see how our own life experiences prove this necessary conclusion to be true.

Our need to love and be loved still lingers, in spite of all the loves we've known.

Our need to be strong keeps us searching for something, or someone, that can hold us together each time our lives start falling apart.

Our need for individual meaning compels us to create one empty purpose after another, pouring our passions into bottomless tasks.

Our need to feel cared for coerces us to accept the cruelty of others in exchange for a bit of their kindness.

It doesn't have to be this way!

Maybe you're wondering, "What do I have to do to find and enter this Inner Kingdom that knows what I need even before I ask?"

Well, you can stop wondering and start your journey right now, right where you are. Start here: let your need grow to know yourself more fully. Allow it to become your guide and nothing can stand in your way.

Your need for a new understanding of yourself, your longing for a higher vision, is coming to you from the Cosmic Destination itself: the Free Mind. From this very moment, find more and more ways to become increasingly conscious of what your true needs are. And then, regardless of the consequences, *accept no substitutes.*

How To Use Your Morning Coffee For A Glimpse Of Your Own Higher Consciousness

Each morning after pouring myself a steaming mug of coffee, I add two teaspoons of sugar to the cup and stir vigorously. Then, as coffee and sugar crystals swirl and mingle into one another, I go to the refrigerator and take out the carton of milk.

When I return to my waiting cup of coffee and look into its steamy depths, I see a semi-dark, opaque surface that appears still. There's no visible movement in the liquid. But all is not as it seems.

As I add the milk, a completely different story unfolds. The moment the milk pours into the cup and flows beneath the coffee's calm surface, a delicious looking vanilla whirlpool appears. Almost as if by magic, my coffee transforms itself into a rich creamy color. Here's what has happened. You might want to try this unique and fun experiment for yourself.

In the few split moments between having stirred in my sugar and getting the milk out of the refrigerator, the surface tension of the coffee in my mug develops sufficiently enough to make the entire contents of my cup appear still. But, just beneath this exposed calm exterior, the coffee is very much in motion.

I've taken the time to tell this story from my kitchen because it helps illustrate some of the dimensions and hidden dynamics of our present level of consciousness; of both the me mind and the Free Mind.

The *surface tension* of my coffee represents our so-called conscious mind, while the *whirling depths* just below it represent our subconscious or unconscious mind. These two layers of mind are really one—they're connected—and yet, just as with the coffee in my mug, *they act independently of one another*. That's why we often find ourselves trapped in a web of our own making before we even know we've been spinning. It's these commonly understood, often tangled, levels of our own intellect that we've named in our study the me mind.

Standing in sharp contrast to this divided mental nature that lives with virtually no understanding of its own operations, the Free Mind is that still-secret part of yourself capable of witnessing the complete actions of the me mind; *while at the same time knowing that its nature has nothing in common with any of the conflict or confusion it may see.* Yes, this state is possible. And in some ways, it's just the beginning.

As you journey along freedom's path, and establish contact with the Free Mind, you'll discover the presence of a higher nature that is to the mechanical, strictly either/or, yes/no thinking of the me mind; what a light switch is to sunlight. What once seemed impossible to you will be your quiet reality to enjoy, including:

1. The discovery of a bright new world above you and, at the same time, the realization that *you are this higher world you've found.*

2. A dynamic self awareness, where intelligence and your actions are one force, free of fear, friction, and any internal conflict.

3. The embrace of a greater life of your own a million light years beyond the usual mind, and yet, as close as the distance between two thoughts.

4. A clear perception of self as being a wave that rolls back into the sea, and that is then neither wave nor sea, but both.

The Free Mind lives far above the mental and emotional tides that are forever pulling on the me mind. This Original Nature can't choose against itself because it's whole. Its silent strength is in its unique "apartness" from the ever-whirling, dizzy world of the me mind.

There are many special advantages in learning how to be apart from what you've always mechanically accepted as yourself. But, we're not talking about acting cold, indifferent, or separating yourself from life. Just the opposite is true.

Living from the Free Mind empowers you to be a part of your own life by making you a grateful and conscious participant in the breathtaking complexity of your own nature.

You enjoy a new relationship with yourself, where instead of being frightened by your own flooding thoughts and feelings, you're eager to know more about them. And this heightened level of involvement in your own life changes the direction of your days in a dramatic way. *Nothing* can pull you down. Let's see why.

The difference between the me mind and the Free Mind is the difference between life on the jungle floor and being in a plane, flying *over* it.

To the individual dwelling in the jungle it appears that he or she has choices. But, in reality, the life choices that arise in the dense undergrowth are really determined by the fierce creatures and clinging vines that also live there. *Choices at this life level are between lion and tiger.* These aren't really choices at all! What difference does it make what a person is running from?

Our selections made from within the dark confines of the me mind are really only hidden circles; painful patterns hidden from sight in the naturally occurring cycle of opposites. Life on the jungle floor is always the same: attack, retreat; attack, retreat. Yes, you stay busy, but also weary from going nowhere. The Free Mind knows how to lift you above anything that lashes at you.

The following true story was shared with a group of students who were meeting to discuss how our true higher needs are blocked by the me mind. As John W. told us all about his amazing experience, everyone gained a better understanding of how the me mind keeps us its confused captives. We also learned all about a surprise solution with the power to take us out of the me mind's jungle of mental opposites, and to deliver us to a higher world where no lions and tigers dwell.

WALK INTO A BRIGHT NEW WORLD JUST OUTSIDE OF YOURSELF

From his introductory remarks to our group that evening, it seemed that John W. was a man who had almost everything. But one of his greatest sources of pride and pleasure was his sophisticated big screen television system. With over one hundred and thirty-two satellite-supplied channels to choose from, including a multi-programmable VCR, John told us he felt a bit like the ruler of his own electronic kingdom: a kind of king in his own mind. And there were good reasons why he felt this way.

With nothing more than the push of a button from one of his four remote controls, John could leap almost anywhere in the world without ever having to move from his favorite chair. But with all this command in his hands, he told us that he still wasn't satisfied. So he added another thirty-two cable channels and one more VCR. But even these new pleasures were short-lived.

Taking us deeper and deeper into his electronic adventure, John reported that more and more of his TV time was spent just wildly flicking from one channel to another. Before his unblinking eyes sports events, movies, and travelogues blurred into one great endless film. And since nothing could please him, the only thing left for him to do was to push the buttons on his TV remote control faster and faster.

Then, late one night, right in the middle of one of his button pushing frenzies, John said something unthinkable happened. *He accidentally pushed the one button that turned all the power off to his equipment.*

There was a crackle, a pop, and everything went black. Silence flooded into the room. All the pulsating images and sounds that filled the room a moment before were sucked back into his giant big screen TV. And then, John continued, came the unexpected.

As stunned as he was by the sudden emptiness, he was also grateful for it. He knew this moment was what he'd been looking for all along, only he just didn't know it! The sweet and sudden silence he was enjoying wasn't listed in the TV or cable guides.

His real need, all along, had been for a quiet moment, but there was no way to find it where his usual mind had him busy looking!

In this short story are dozens of valuable insights into both the nature of the me mind and the Free Mind. Also found within John's truthful tale are several glimpses about some more of the Free Mind's amazing powers. Let's review three of the more important points.

1. John assumed he was unhappy because he couldn't find the right show to watch on his big screen. And it was this mistaken thinking, right up until the time of his fortunate accident, that kept him searching in vain through the same field of empty choices.

2. Only after the power went off did John realize that what he really wanted was something his usual mind hadn't even thought of as an option! It was silence he longed for.

3. The whole time John spent feeling frustrated and dissatisfied, there was a superior alternative available to him if he could have seen outside of himself to consider it.

John had been a captive of the invisible and vicious loop that is the root of the me mind. This lower nature can't see that its own escape plans come to it from *the same level of the captive: itself!*

For example the me mind loves to dream of a new relationship that will be better than the one just failed. But even as it lays its plans for a new romance, this unhappy nature can't see that the principle reason the last involvement shattered was because it drove it apart with its unrealistic expectations; demands which always begin with, "you must satisfy me!"

Pressure in any relationship—even if its purpose is to try and hold things together—always drives it apart. We can learn to do better than to allow ourselves to be directed by this misguided me mind. We can learn to step outside of its self defeating operations.

TAKE THIS UNCOMMON ACTION AND CHANGE YOUR EVERYDAY EXPERIENCE

Imagine for a moment you've gone to one of these new, huge cineplexes that have eight separate theaters. You buy your ticket and walk into the show you came to see. But, before too long, you realize you don't like what's on the screen so you decide to change theaters. Unfortunately, the next movie's just as pointless. So you change theaters again. And again.

Now as long as you remain one of those movie audience members who live only from the level of the me

34

mind, you're only choice is to ramble around within the cineplex. You move from one show to the next—all the while not remembering that the film you just walked into was unable to please you *the first time you saw it*.

But living from the Free Mind, another choice comes to you. *You walk out of the movies. You take yourself out of the theater complex*. Now you're free to go enjoy the rest of your day in some other way.

To help you better grasp the intention of this parallel illustration, we need to take a brief look into the theater of our usual mind.

Consider your own thinking for just a moment. Can you see how your mind loves to go over and over events that haven't even happened yet? This mental process is the me mind hard at work. But let's take a closer look at what this little nature of ours is really doing.

Each time the me mind envisions some future event, it's actually trying to find a feeling of security for itself. But the only security this lower nature can ever know is *imaginary*. So it has to dream up one scene after another where somehow you'll come out a winner.

But, the more victories it conjures up in this way, the more fear it feels that it won't win the battles *it* just created. And the more agitated this low level of mind becomes from its own unconscious activity, the more it tries to settle itself with more mental movies. We can see the end of this painful picture without having to draw it ourselves. This psychological profile demonstrates what it means to be both prisoner and prison maker!

The Free Mind is always a witness to your whole mental and emotional experience, so it can't be made a slave of any hidden desire. In this instance, the higher intelligence of the Free Mind instantly understands that no mere mental picture of security has any real power to make you feel secure. And this realization empowers you, effortlessly, *to just walk out of your own mental movie.* Can you see the immense difference between the me mind and the Free Mind scenarios?

Being able to consciously walk out of the movie-making complex of the me mind is the same as the power to free yourself. Why? Because once you walk out of this tiny darkened theater that your lower nature considers the whole world, you know for certain and at last: *there is something outside the world of your usual mind.* And once you walk into its light, you know that everything can be forever new for you.

From this day forward, be a careful observer of the moving pictures in your own mind. Learn to watch all the various scenes without casting yourself as any of the players on the screen. Remember, nothing you see in that darkened theater is who you really are. Use these ten truths that summarize this chapter to help keep you awake.

1. Settle it completely in your mind: You're going to be free to choose the life you want.

2. You can only be as free as you're willing to see the extent of your inner captivity.

3. When inwardly challenged to come to any fear-filled decision, never let yourself forget that struggling to get *more* of what hasn't brought you happiness can't possibly make you any more happy.

4. The day will come when you'll no more mistake yourself for one of your own thoughts than you'd confuse an eagle for a cuckoo.

5. Before we can change the kind of events we experience in our lives, we must first change our own nature, for we never attract anything to ourselves other than what we are.

6. To catch the false self in the act of stealing your life, just quietly notice how it can't stop thinking, or talking, about the very thing it says it can't stand.

7. Being captive of fear is always senseless so, to free yourself, just catch the false self creating the conditions in your mind where that fear seems reasonable.

8. Like the light of a single candle cuts through the darkest night, your true need to be free is far more powerful than any shadow of doubt.

9. Just as the roots of a fragrant flower must find the right soil for that flower to reach its full bloom, so we too need contact with a Higher Ground.

10. There is no substitution for the realization of the Free Mind.

Here's a helpful exercise you'll want to call upon over and over again. Watch how its healing influence brightens and lightens your days. Practicing this new action will put the power of the Free Mind to work for you. Inner freedom follows.

Make a practice of catching yourself in front of the "big screen." One way to know you're sitting in the front row of the me mind is to detect negative feelings that imply there's nothing that can be done about the way you feel at the moment. Fear, anger, depression, and frustration are a few of the inner conflicts that the me mind loves to project through your psychic system.

At the moment you catch these mental crooks stealing your life within the darkness of that mental movie, remember that you always have a higher option. Instead of looking for another self-created scene better than the one you're in, call on the Free Mind by deliberately taking your mind off of the mental screen of thoughts before you. *Wake yourself up!* Here's a good place to start.

Notice the tension in your hands, or the feel and temperature of the air around you. Become conscious of the expression on your face. Listen to the sound of your own voice as you speak.

Placing your attention in the fully present moment helps to snap whatever psychic spell you may have been under. Your wish to be awake and free, coupled with your new level of awareness, is the same as walking out of the theater all together.

Now, once you're out, do your best to stay out! Allow the sunlight of your own momentarily awakened nature to gently warm you. Let the Free Mind remind you of what real pleasures are. You'll want more and more sunlight, and less and less of the me mind's dark back stage dramatics.

CHAPTER 3

The Secret Of Living Thought Free

IN THE COMPETITIVE AND COMPLEX WORLDS OF BUSINESS and science, imagination is critical to the processes of creativity. It serves a valuable and practical purpose. New developments are created by imagining better ways to improve old technologies. Important developments come in increments. Progress moves ahead one step at a time.

But in our inner life, we don't want a continuation of *what has been*. We want the *new*, and the *free*. We don't want to repeat ourselves or build on patterns that contain obvious limitations.

This means to succeed in our search for self liberation we must proceed in a completely different manner than the world around us would recognize. We are bound to set our compass *not by what we wish to find, but by what we know we must leave behind us*.

Awakening to our own True Nature is a process of *letting go*. This point is a significant one. We don't set out for what is limitless. Instead we quietly detect and reject those aspects of ourselves whose presence prevents us from enjoying the unrestrained life. As we let go of these invisible anchors, we find ourselves effortlessly rising towards the silent and ever-expansive nature of the Free Mind.

But again, we mustn't try and imagine what our lives would be like living from this new nature. As our own experiences have shown us many times over, the pictures we create in our minds never live up to our expectations. And this is particularly true when it comes to the flattering images we hold of ourselves.

For example, we've all known those terrible moments in life where the picture we have of ourselves, as being strong enough to deal with whatever happens to us, suddenly falls off the wall and shatters before our unbelieving eyes. And we're left standing there, stunned at how we could have been so blind to ourselves!

So, we must make this clear. What we want is that freedom, those strengths that are based *in reality*. And to achieve these reality-based powers, we must seek them there: within what is *real*.

And yet, over the years of teaching these principles of self liberation, I've learned that the subject of *reality* is not exactly a welcome one. It seems most of us have little interest in facing what feels like the harsh light of our individual existence. It's not difficult to understand why.

Our lives seem to flicker, like a bulb that may or may not light up the next instant. One moment we shine, the next moment what was once a glow is barely a flickering possibility. In that sometimes fading light, we see all too much about ourselves that seems shallow or loveless. We're frightened that life itself may be too bleak and cruel to withstand. And soon, the *fear* of what we see as being the reality of life, *becomes the basis of our reality*.

This fear-filled mindset leaves us but little hope. We're reduced to looking for, and finding, the happiness we long for only in our hopes and dreams. And so it goes that our lives become based in tomorrow. How else can it be for us? For in the way we look at what we think is reality, *today just can't be all there is!*

But the day to day existence we all find so hard to face without our dreams of escape is not *real life*. We only *think* it's real. And the only reason for this erroneous experience of reality is because we're still experiencing the whole of our lives *in thought*.

We are not intended to *think* our way through this life of ours. The overwhelming evidence of this truth is all around us, only we've lost the innate ability to see it.

ABANDON YOUR USUAL WAYS OF THINKING

Imagine for a moment you're driving home from work, or wherever, and that you've just come from having a pretty rough day. As you drive along, your eyes see the road before you, but your mind is in the past. It's very busy re-running all of the days unpleasant events.

Over and over again, you feel that painful stab of some thoughtless remark someone cruelly blurted out, or the embarrassment of that stupid comment you made without thinking. And with each mental replay of this unpleasant scene, you go deeper and deeper into thought, desperately trying to find a way to escape what seems an intolerable situation.

But what you don't see happening to you is that *the more you think, the more you sink!* Exactly the opposite of what you think you're accomplishing. And the deeper you sink in thought, the less you're able to see what the rest of you is doing.

Driving reckless, speeding, missing the exit you want—these, and other equally dangerous stunts, are only a few of the foolish things that happen to you while driving under the influence of a stream of self compromising, self wrecking thoughts.

Your life, in moments such as these, is actually out of your hands. It belongs to your thinking, to the me mind. This undeveloped nature doesn't understand what it's doing to itself, or to you, as it struggles to find a way out from under the weight of *its own unconscious actions*.

What the me mind doesn't understand is that freedom is a state of being; *the relief it seeks can never be a creation of thought*. But there's good reason for this lower nature's ignorance, as well as for its covert efforts to keep us asleep in a similar state.

The me mind is out of business the moment we wake up to realize that *free is what we are* each time we can catch ourselves about to build another prison out of thought. Our awakened awareness instantly cancels our captivity. And as our self created bondage fades, *so does our desperate need to escape!* What the me mind doesn't want us to know is that we're *already* free.

THE FREE MIND IS FULLY RESPONSIBLE

The purpose of all True Teachings has always been to help make us aware that seeking the Higher Life through mind-made ideals is like trying to row a raft to the stars. Once this understanding is clear, we no longer spend our vital energies trying to think ourselves into some happiness or greatness as we conceive it.

Christ often spoke of the futility of using thought as a foundation for knowing our True Self. He asked in countless ways, "What man, taking thought, can add one cubit to his stature?" He taught his disciples to "take no thought for the morrow."

Christ knew the great need for awakening his disciples to the realization that a life spent in only the mental realm was one of secret and sad captivity. And yet, as significant as His teachings may have been in days passed, they are meaningless to us today unless we're able to discover, for ourselves, the freedom and fearlessness of the thought-free life. Can such a lofty life level be attained? Yes!

Please understand that we're not talking about giving up and living an empty, thoughtless life. No, we're not. But this is exactly what the me mind will whisper to us in its secretly worried, self serving thoughts. Besides, we'll never truly convince ourselves that to be anxious or stressed out is what it means to be thoughtful or caring. There's just no such thing as "caring" ourselves apart!

To live from the Free Mind *does not* mean to live thoughtlessly or to abandon our real responsibilities. Just the opposite is true. Some of the greatest men and women who have ever lived drew their inspiration and direction from the silent strength of the Free Mind.

In his book *The Power of Your Supermind*, Vernon Howard tells his readers about several of these unique individuals. "Enlightened men are often accused of being impractical dreamers. Research proves otherwise. Henry David Thoreau, considered an idler by some, was a highly practical merchant in his pencil and graphite firm. Plato was a successful salesman to his Egyptian customers. Jacob Boehme, in addition to being claimed as a mystical genius, was known in his native Gorlitz as a master businessman and shoemaker. John Burroughs, the American nature philosopher, was an efficient bank examiner."

The Secret Liberating Power Of
Self Observation

"I want to know if it's really possible to live a thought-free life. The whole idea of being able to live without second thoughts about myself is very appealing. What do I need to know to get started?"

Here's where we meet an important friend and ally of the Free Mind. Just as a gold miner far beneath the earth needs special lamps and tools to shed light on ore-rich rocks, we too need a way to see into the darkened inner world of our own psyche. To illuminate our inner world and work, we need to learn about *self observation*.

"How does it work?"

We've already learned that we're captives of a false nature, a self of sorts, created by our own whirling thoughts and feelings. To free ourselves from this imposter nature and its imposed reality, *we are called to see that its world is not the same as ours*. This discovery begins with the conscious action of deliberately *stepping back from our thoughts*. We become an observer of ourselves, watchful of both the content—and the intent—of everything arising from our own mind and heart.

"What do you mean, step back from my thoughts? That would be a good trick! Where do I start?"

Right where you are. In fact, let's begin this very moment. Become aware, right now, *without thinking* about it, that you are thinking. *See* that there are thoughts and feelings coursing through you. As you watch their movements, be their silent witness. Just observe.

"I believe I've heard of this practice before, and I can readily understand its benefits. But I seem unable to really apply the principles to my own life. Can you help?"

To observe yourself, assume no position on the thoughts and feelings you see moving through you. Don't put yourself on either side of any thought's content. In other words, *be neither for nor against any thought with any other thought*. And should you get temporarily caught in the web of any thinking, then *watch that event* with the impartial intent and simply start over. Just let your awareness of these thoughts and feelings be there.

The foundation of self observation is a higher self awareness that puts you in direct contact with a new and superior Intelligence, a silent wisdom that immediately goes to work in your favor. This initial level of the Free Mind knows exactly what to do with all that passes before it. It can see the mindless, self serving antics of the me mind coming from a thousand miles away, which is the same as taking you out of harm's way. For this elevated nature, incisive actions are effortless, and require no thought.

"Please tell me, exactly how can self observation cancel self compromise?"

ABOLISH HARMFUL INNER VOICES

Look closely for all of the inner gold locked within the wisdom of the following fact. Your extra efforts here will pay off handsomely.

If you can't *see* some thought or feeling as it goes through you, then you *don't have the choice whether to be that thought or feeling or not*.

So, before we can choose not to compromise ourselves, we must first become acutely aware of those thoughts of ours that may be holding some secret seed of self defeat. If we don't know we're doing this kind of compromised thinking—or acting out their emotional counterparts—what else can follow but to receive the defeat that they embody?

For example, these harmful inner voices and emotional forces may tell us to resent someone or to hate our life; or to give up, and accept fear as a way of life. Our own thoughts may instruct us, without our ever knowing it, to cling to doubts; or to jump headlong into pools of self pity. And because we don't know there's any alternative, we do as we're instructed.

What we don't know *yet*, but what we're learning even now, is that we can wake up right in the middle of these mental ordeals. Working with self observation, we can actually *see*, for ourselves, that these self compromising thoughts are just that: *thoughts*. They have no real authority, which means their unconscious direction does not have to be our destiny.

"I've had a few moments being aware of my own thoughts, but it doesn't seem to me like anything's happening when I watch. And there have been other times when I felt very uncomfortable with what I saw within myself. What should I do?"

Just keep going.

Your persistent wish to silently watch your own thoughts and feelings *cannot be denied*. So have no concern that your initial efforts to be self observing may not reveal that much about yourself. Which brings us to an important point. Never mistake any discovery *about* yourself for being yourself. This is one of the favorite tricks of the me mind. In other words, don't look at your present level of insight, whatever it may be, as being a negative. Instead, observe it as a fact that's *for you*, not against you. Patient investigation of any temporary truth about yourself can only bring more light into your inner world. Greater and greater inner vision will come, but you must grow accustomed to this self illumination. And this includes what happens *within you* as the light of self observation brightens.

There are many mistaken notions dwelling there in the darkness of the me mind. To think they won't squeal as you bring this light to bear on them would be naive on your part. But, with the persistent practice of self observation, you can even learn to use the me mind's howling to live thought free. Here's how.

To begin with, always take a conscious step back from anything which howls at you from within. Once removed in this special fashion, now see that any shriek of discomfort, worry, anxiety, or shame, *can never be a part of who you really are*. The Free Mind has always known this secret. It's time for you to realize the freedom in this discovery. It can be done. Others have gone before you.

The High Ground of the Free Mind is quietly waiting for you. Step up and into this thought-free realm by allowing the following three higher facts to help you develop your practice of self observation.

1. Casually, but definitely, consciously defy any feeling that tells you you're stuck with it.

2. Stepping back from your own thoughts and learning to watch them is the same as stepping up to the Free Mind.

3. Being receptive to a Higher fact about yourself lifts you to the level of that insight where the fact you once feared no longer frightens you, just as eagles don't fear sharks.

LEAVE ANY TROUBLED THOUGHT
RIGHT WHERE YOU FIND IT

At one time I lived in a beautiful part of California called Ojai. The upper Ojai Valley is filled with huge walnut and oak trees that stand out against a backdrop of scrub and high chaparral.

The seasons are marked by the changing native grasses and flowers. Each year begins in purple clover and white apricot blossoms, followed by seas of wild yellow mustard. Then come the endless green fields of wild oats which slowly turn tan. And, if you know where to look, you can find clear, perennial streams and pools that swell with the spring rains.

One of my greatest pleasures was the freedom to disappear into the nearby mountains to walk along these streams. I enjoyed climbing in their stony beds, hopping from rock to rock. There was always so much to take in and, I must admit, sometimes I did more than just take in the special atmosphere. If I was lucky, I'd spot an especially knurly piece of walnut or manzanita, or an exceptional stone, and take it home with me.

One afternoon I was quite a ways into the hills following a rain-swollen stream, when I saw it: a fist-sized rock whose colors were unlike any I'd ever seen before. It lay partially submerged in the stream. In a moment or two, I reached its secret hiding place and was holding it in my hands. Another treasure to take pleasure in I thought to myself as I turned to head back home.

Forty-five minutes later I placed my newest natural wonder on a wide, old wooden bench, next to a small collection of bonsai trees just outside my back door. It fit in well with my eclectic collection of odds and ends from the mountains. Then, making sure everything was in its right place for the last time, I went inside.

The next morning when I got up and went outside to admire my unusual find, what a shock was waiting for me. Where just the day before had sat an almost luminescent stone now squatted a dull, lifeless rock. It was as though it had somehow died overnight. In another instant, I realized exactly what had happened.

The stone's beauty was gone because it no longer had the stream's water running over it to keep it sparkling. It was dry and dehydrated. No moisture, no shine; no shine, no glory. In that moment, the mistake I had made was clear, and I knew I would never make it again. That rock belonged where I had found it in the stream. That's where it should have been left.

This simple outdoor story holds important inner lessons for us on many levels, but one stands out from the rest. Even though they may sparkle at first glance, *learn to leave troubling thoughts and feelings where you find them.*

For example, why pick up that bad feeling that always attends someone else's careless remark, just because it momentarily attracts your attention? *You don't have to take it home with you. Just leave it where you find it.*

Why wait until your mind is broiling to realize, that while negative thoughts seem to be teeming with life, what they really are is a form of psychic parasites. Leave all such dark forms where you find them, in the mud of the me mind. That's where they should stay.

To further develop this important study, let's review a general mental inventory of other thoughts and feelings better off left where we find them. The more we know about the content and presence of our own thoughts, the easier it will be to not pick up the ones that turn our lives ugly.

1. Comparing yourself to others, or even to your own past performances, serves no purpose other than to torment. *Leave all comparative thoughts right where you find them.*

   Special Idea To Ponder: *The Free Mind is beyond any measurement.*

2. Avoid picking up any thought or feeling that instructs you to give yourself away today so that in some tomorrow you might own yourself. *Leave all anxious thoughts and feelings right where you find them.*

   Special Idea To Ponder: *The Free Mind knows you already have what you need to be happy right now.*

3. Angry people want you to feel their fire. If you refuse to pick up their self punishing state, they're left with its burning. That's what they need—and much better for you. *Leave the fury of others right where you find it.*

   Special Idea To Ponder: *The Free Mind recognizes all forms of hatred and resentment as being self wrecking.*

4. Never pick up any thought that claims your defeat in life is a fact. Defeat only becomes a fact of life when you start believing that some temporary dark feeling is your future. Leave all weary thoughts and feelings right where you find them.

   Special Idea To Ponder: *The Free Mind dwells in a world where there's no such thing as defeat.*

5. Before you can ever begin to think of yourself as a victim, you had to have first been victimized by an unseen, punishing thought. *Leave punishing thoughts right where you find them.* Then you won't feel the need to find someone to blame for the way you've made yourself feel.

Special Idea To Ponder: *The Free Mind knows the me mind can't live without wanting to know why everything always happens to it!*

Imagine for a moment what your life might be like if you never again were to pick up a complaining thought or feeling. Think of how your days would flow without carrying the additional weight of those inner voices always telling you, "I'm too tired," or "This is too much for me!" The weight of the world would be replaced by a new sense of freedom. Fresh, new energies would flow.

If this is the kind of inwardly carefree life you really want, then look closely into these next two ideas that together tell one story of freedom: *leaving troubled thoughts right where you find them is the same as not picking up what troubles you.* And if you can leave just one of these weary thoughts behind you, then you can leave two, and three, and four, and fifty!

THE SECRET OF KNOWING WITHOUT THINKING

Most people tend to worry that if they don't worry, something bad will happen to them. But what they don't see is that these worried thoughts they've picked up by mistake are the very storm they fear will come!

When presented with healing, new ideas, such as the ones we're now discovering about the thought-free life, the first thing these individuals ask is, "But what happens if I make a mistake? How can you tell which thoughts and feelings are the right ones to leave where you find them, and which ones do you pick up? What if I choose wrong?"

The Free Mind never worries about such questions! And you needn't either. Here's why. There's a way to know, without ever having to think about it, exactly which of your own thoughts and feelings are your friends, and which are foes, a totally thought-free way to understand which of your thoughts are practical and necessary for everyday life, and which are stealing your life with unsuspected self compromise. It's true. You possess unsuspected powers of perception just waiting to be awakened. The following technique will help you get started with this awakening of the Free Mind.

Set this book down for a minute and allow your eyes to fall on something familiar in the space where you are. Notice how your mind immediately gives that object a name. Having done this part of the exercise, keep your attention on whatever you've selected, and then continue to watch how more thoughts come into your mind about what you're seeing.

Now, while you're witnessing *both* that object *and* your growing stream of associative thoughts and feelings about it, *just drop these thoughts and feelings.*

You can still see the object, and you still know what it is—but now you are *knowing without thinking.* This is your introduction to an unconditioned relationship with life: the beginning of your life in the Free Mind.

In this form of higher attention, of knowing without thinking, you can see that the *meaning* of the object before you has not changed. The difference is that now its meaning speaks directly, silently to you—*instead of you listening to your thoughts tell you about its meaning.*

When it comes to seeing a chair or a pencil, this new kind of thought-free state may not seem too profound. But this practice can, and should, be enlarged to encompass your whole life.

The benefits behind the ability to understand something, or someone, without having to go into thought, cannot be over estimated. One small example reveals how this special power bestows you with a new kind of self safety.

The only time we can get hurt by another person or by some event is when we've somehow fallen into a wrong relationship with them. Wrong relationships are the root of painful dependency. And we couldn't be wrongly connected to anyone or anything, *if* we were able to *see*, ahead of time, what entering into and being within this relationship *really* meant.

After an important relationship has failed, how many times have we said to ourselves something like: "I only wish I knew back then what I know now!" It's worth mentioning that the only thing this 20-20 hindsight really does is make the me mind think it can see. But, it can't. *Thoughts can't see.*

And that's why, all too often, we don't see the writing on the wall until after that wall has fallen over on us! But the only reason we can't see that any wall is about to fall is because our eyes just don't want to see a wobbly wall. What they do see is a wall of our own seemingly solid thoughts *about what we want that wall to be: a wall built upon an idea about what we have to have to feel secure, cared for, or happy.*

It may be a little humbling, but it's not hard to name some of the things *we want to see*:

1. We look for someone who has a strength we can't seem to find in ourselves.

2. We search for some situation in which we can remain secure.

3. We seek a pleasure that won't turn into its painful opposite.

But the freeing facts are we're never betrayed by any situation, nor by any other person who we hoped would be strong for us, but who turns out to be weak, cruel, or underhanded.

No. The real betrayal is always when we listen, without question, to our own mind tell us we need another's approval in order to feel secure, or to succeed.

We're betrayed each time we pick up the false idea that there's strength in numbers; so now we must find a way to make ourselves fit in, *if* we want to feel safe.

These mistaken, and ultimately self betraying, walls of thought—and all others like them—*have to fall*. They're not real. The Free Mind is a life without any such walls, and without all of their falls.

If the sole cause of our conflict is in our psychic carelessness, because we unknowingly pick up and carry home with us self compromising thoughts and feelings, then the solution we need and should seek, *must be in a new kind of awareness*. And this Higher Awareness *does* exist in a Free Mind. We need only align ourselves with its powers, which can be done.

Practice knowing without thinking. Begin today. *Right now.*

Let yourself see the meaning of individuals and their actions, of your behavior, of world events, of all your relationships—*without* telling yourself what you see. Again, let the meaning of what is before you *reveal itself to you*. Keep *you* out of it. If you don't, then self compromising self interest will come into and cloud the picture.

Bravely go through your day in this new way. Switch back and forth between your natural need for practical thought, as required in your business or home life, and this new state of seeing, of knowing without thinking. Be patient with yourself. For a while you may feel as though you just have to pick up some thought or feeling, even though a part of you knows you shouldn't. Just learn to watch all of that too. And when you fail, try your best not to pick up self judgmental thoughts.

And lastly, *don't fear anything you may see in yourself, or anywhere else.* Don't pick up these feelings either. They just want to load you down with a false sense of self borne out of an equally false sense of responsibility. *No* fear belongs to you, now or ever. The Free Mind *knows* this. And it knows what to do about all other forms of disturbance—*all without thinking.* Let it tell you what you need to know, and one day you'll know what it means to live fully, safely, and securely from the Free Mind.

Being truly receptive requires a quiet mind, so try and find the secret lessons about self silence within each of the following ten points. Your discoveries will put you on the road to living without any second thoughts about yourself.

1. The riches of the Free Mind never fade and can't be stolen.

2. Choosing your daily direction from a confused mind is like using the blades of a blender for a compass.

3. Catching yourself about to pick up a compromising thought and then leaving it where you found it, is like putting a piece of gold in your pocket.

4. You don't have to be in your own life the way you think you do.

5. Come awake as often as you can to the difference between seething and soothing thoughts.

6. The "feeling" of yourself is to "being" yourself what a wind is to the open sky.

7. The Free Mind knows fully the me mind, but the me mind knows nothing of freedom.

8. There is nothing more practical than the practice of *knowing without thinking*.

9. As often as possible, remember to just quietly let go of any thought or feeling that troubles you—*including* any ensuing thought that threatens you with more trouble should you dare let that first thought go.

10. The emergence of the Free Mind takes special effort, while those disturbances within the me mind take none.

TAKE THIS BOLD STEP TOWARDS LIVING THOUGHT FREE

Each morning, before you launch into your usual routine, find someplace where you can sit quietly by yourself for about ten minutes. If you have to get up earlier to make this time for yourself, *then just do it. Use this time to do nothing except to be conscious of how your own mind refuses to join you in doing nothing.*

But, *don't* work at this attempt to be thought free. Instead, just silently observe how your thoughts won't stand still; see just how thought "full" you really are. Again, your aim *is not* to "do" something with these ten minutes, but *see* something about yourself during them. This is healthy self acquaintance.

Let your growing awareness that these tumbling thoughts *have a life of their own* serve as your first step in separating yourself from their influence. This is the marvelous beginning of self silence. Up until now, you may have never questioned the notion your thoughts didn't really belong to you. Now you can begin to witness this fact.

This exercise will help you see that your Real Nature is *not* any of those thoughts passing through you. Living without thoughts about yourself isn't far behind this inner discovery.

CHAPTER 4

Learn How To Take Yourself To A Higher, Happier Life Level

Human beings are a unique creation in the cosmic scheme of things. And it's very important for our studies of the Free Mind to clarify the nature of this special distinction. Unlike the untold billions of other life forms teaming on the Earth—whose nature is an open and shut case—human nature is *not fixed*. What does this mean to you? Only everything!

The tiger, the horse, and the bird, *must express* their nature. They have no *real* choice. And even though they may be free to choose which part of the jungle, or open range, in which they want to feed and roam, these animals have no choice as to *the kind of world in which they must dwell*.

The tiger can't choose to live above the jungle floor any more than a shark can decide to soar through blue skies. The tiger, horse, bird, and shark, must live *where* they do because of *what* they are. Try to see this deeply.

The tiger's nature determines its life. And that life is *a part of the jungle floor*. They are inseparable. The tiger's nature and its *life level* are one thing. The tiger's life level determines the world it *must* inhabit. Its nature and life level are as fixed as a leopards spots.

But your nature is not fixed. This is spiritual fact. And now you must turn this powerful fact into your discovery and personal experience.

You *do* have the freedom to choose the kind of world you call your own. Why spend your life in a steamy jungle of roaring thoughts, or in a dark valley filled with sad and worried emotions when, by *choosing higher*, you can live happier? Your days can be as cool and relaxed as a clear mountain stream, *if* you decide that's the life you want.

But, decide you must. What very few men and women ever come to realize, spiritually speaking, is that life is a ceaseless series of inner choices about where they want to live. And even though we may not fully understand the nature of these choices, or why they must be made, *to not choose* is to lose. Here's why.

The complete range of life-level possibilities, from the conflict-filled jungle floor to the serene mountain-top, all exist right within your own uninvestigated nature. And to not choose the upward path through this life is to resign yourself to the laws of gravity—which always choose in favor of their own nature: *down*.

A mental picture will help bring some of these important invisible concepts into clearer view.

Imagine a huge mansion with unlimited floors. Now further envision that each floor in this mansion represents one life level out of all of the countless possibilities. If it's helpful, think of this mansion as representing your True Nature, the Free Mind.

But, to bring our illustration down to earth, think of the largest department store you've ever shopped. Like the mansion in our mental picture, each floor of the department store displays and offers items peculiar only to it. You won't find guns and ammo sold on the same floor as books of learning; nor do you find automotive supplies where delicate lace is displayed. And so, in much the same way, the level of each of the floors in our inner mansion determine the life choices available on it.

For instance, as long as you live in the basement of this mansion, you can't choose to enjoy the unrestricted cool air and natural sunlight of the first floor resting just above it. Similarly, on the second floor you can't choose to see the beauty and panorama of the view that only the fifth floor and higher can offer. And so on it goes, all the way to higher and higher floors.

Your life experiences are determined by which of these "floors" you dwell upon. This means that each floor represents a possible life level. But, while each of these inner levels and the natural events attracted to them may be fixed, *you are not*. Unlike the tiger that can't leave the land of the tiger, you can leave any troubling part of your own present nature far behind you. Read on to discover one more amazing feature of your True Nature.

Picture a set of stairs that winds its way up and through this immense inner mansion. These steps start in the darkened basement and lead up until they go out of sight. Each step of the staircase is also a part of your True Nature, but *none of them belongs to any one floor-level through which they pass*.

This means you don't have to remain on any level not of your choosing. *You have the power to climb.* You can change your life experiences by walking away from any of those unwanted worlds within you that create your unpleasant days. In this way, self departure is the same as self elevation. Your life is meant to be an upward journey.

Be The Ruler Of Your Own Reactions

There is one power of the Free Mind you *already* possess which can not only build a ladder that reaches from one life level to the next, but this same power helps you climb that ladder so you may enter each successive realm. What is this secret strength at the source of self elevation? *You can learn.*

These three words—*I can learn*—are the most powerful three words in any language. Nothing in the universe can hold down that rare individual who clearly realizes that he or she *doesn't know* what's in the way of his or her happiness, but *who is willing to find out*. If painful patterns are prisons without walls, then a willingness to learn the new and the True is the same as a gateway to freedom.

From my book The Secret Way of Wonder, we learn that the me mind knows of only two possible ways to turn when faced with a personal crisis. But we also find out that neither of the directions it knows to look in ever resolve anything. "Whenever painful events happen, they tend to fall on only one of two sides of a person. The first side is the denial side. When turning this way, refusal rules. Regret, self pity and endless explanations generally follow. Or, the life blow falls on the angry side where the turning is to burning. Resentment rages. Hatred and feelings of betrayal mushroom into self righteous plans for avenging the wrong. But what both these sad sides have in common is that they keep the person between them a victim—turning in vain from one side to the other—only to find nothing changes except for the kind of pain found there."

But there exists a third way to turn, a superior choice that leads to a higher life level where neither confusion, conflict, nor crisis is found. I call this higher direction "Turning To Learning."

"I must confess, there are times when my personal difficulties are overwhelming. I'd love to learn a new way to face these crises and feel confident everything will work out in my favor. What exactly does it mean to 'turn in a learning direction'? What would I have to do?"

Turning to learning begins with the honest recognition that our present approach to solving personal problems just doesn't work.

"Well, that's not too hard to admit, but what's to be gained in conceding that I seem to be stuck?"

This may come as a surprise. Learning to live without recurring problems begins with losing faith in our habitual responses that tell us how to be free of them.

"How could loss of faith in myself ever be seen as a needed gain? What I need is more confidence, not less!"

Losing confidence in your own heated, or heavy-hearted, reactions does *not* mean that you have to see yourself in a disparaging light, any more than stepping out of the way of a runaway truck would make you think of yourself as a coward.

"Yes, but what do getting out of the way of a truck and losing faith in my own reactions have to do with one another? I thought we were looking for a superior way to deal with personal crisis situations?"

We are! Let's look a little closer. We let the runaway truck pass us by because we know it's only a mindless machine. We realize it can't recognize the danger its own undirected nature represents. Now follow closely. We must learn to let our own habitual reactions roll by us because, just like the wild truck, these reactions of ours are mechanical in nature. And since we know that *machines can't learn*, this means *neither will we learn what is really needed to free ourselves*, as long we allow our reactions to lead the way.

"I never thought of my reactions as being in the way of my growth, but what can take their place? If I don't react to my problems as they pop up, then what do I do in the moment of crisis?"

Don't you see? *You'll learn!* To learn means *to discover*. Now learn this: reactions never reveal, they conceal. Remaining under the rule of any reaction limits your choices in life to only the direction *that reaction gives you* to take. But the key point is this: no reaction-supplied direction can ever lead anywhere higher than the level of the reaction. If these mechanical responses actually knew as much as they pretend to, we wouldn't be repeating the patterns that always lead us back to the same kind of personal problems. It should be clear. Our mechanical reactions are at the root of our persistent problems, *and not the way out of them.*

"All this may be true, in fact, I'm sure it probably is, but I have some concerns. What if what's required of me in some moment of crisis is more than I know how to handle? What happens if I let my usual reactions go by, and then find myself unable to learn what I must do?"

Don't give this mistaken concern of the me mind a second thought. *You will learn.* The whole process of self liberation through higher learning is under definite spiritual laws. The very act of turning away from the me mind's mechanical reactions is the same as facing in the direction of the Free Mind. You'll find that who you really are is an endless learning ground, a limitless possibility for higher and higher self discovery.

Swiss poet and theologian Johann Lavater, one of the early pioneers in the science of physiognomy, knew all about the amazing powers of turning to learning. "He who always seeks more light the more he finds, and finds more the more he seeks, is one of the few happy mortals who take and give in every point of time. The tide and ebb of giving and receiving is the sum of human happiness, which he alone enjoys who always wishes to acquire new knowledge, and always finds it."

One last word on this important subject of turning to learning. We all know many men and women who think they already know everything. They're in great spiritual danger that they can't see, but that we must make visible for ourselves. False self certainty is an invisible form of self stagnation.

All that needs to be said about these unhappy individuals can be summed up in a simple, but pointed question author Vernon Howard once asked a small group of his students: "If you *know* so much, why do you suffer the way you do?"

Truthful self inquiry, in the form of such frank self questioning as this, is ultimately healing. Yes, it's strong medicine, to be sure. But before we arbitrarily throw it out, ignore it, or view it as being negative, let's learn why it's wise to place such an uncompromising question before ourselves.

Asking ourselves the truth about our own hidden inner condition, at just the right moments, causes the false certainty created by our strong reactions to fade. Temporary, *but necessary*, self uncertainty follows. And yes, this is good. The unique nature of this conscious uncertainty creates a conscious receptivity, like opening a special inner window through which the refreshing breeze of learning can enter. *Real certainty* is carried in on this gentle wind. Welcome it.

ELEVEN LAWS THAT LIFT YOU TO THE NEXT LIFE LEVEL

If we're ever to succeed in rising above ourselves, we must consider that what we think we already know about freedom may be the cause of our psychic captivity. A little logic reveals a big discovery:

1. We *do* what we *know*.

2. We *get* what we *do*.

3. Therefore, what we *get* from life, what we receive in each of our moments, is a *direct reflection* of our present level of understanding.

Using a slightly different spin, here's the same idea, only more to the point: *the only thing that holds us down is what we don't yet know about ourselves.* This insight explains why our ability to learn the truth about ourselves, to increase our level of self understanding, is the same as being empowered to raise our own life level.

If we want to grow inwardly, free ourselves from the ties that bind, we must find new ways to learn the truth about ourselves—and our lives—that haven't been compromised by the me mind. These higher discoveries call for higher learning. If it helps, look upon this important part of your inner education as a way to better understand what's been keeping you from learning.

Think of each of the following eleven laws as individual magic strands of a flying carpet. Make it your aim to weave them together in your mind. Then watch how these lessons combine to effortlessly lift you to the next higher and happier life level.

The First Law

Nothing can stop you from starting over.

The greatest power you possess for succeeding in life is your understanding that life gives you a fresh start any moment you choose to start fresh. Nothing that stood in your way even a heartbeat before stands there now in the same way. It's all *new*, even if you can't as yet see it that way. You've only to test the truth of this fact about the newness of life to discover the incredible freedom that waits for you just behind it. And then nothing can stop you. You'll know the real secret and the perfect power of starting over.

The Second Law

Don't be afraid to see when something doesn't work.

Learn to be sensitive and to listen to the inner signals that try and tell you when something isn't working. You know what they are. Frustration and resentment to name just a few. The presence of these emotional troubles aren't trying to tell you that you *can't* succeed, only that the road you've insisted upon taking so far doesn't lead where you want. Learning to admit when something isn't working is the same as teaching yourself what will.

The Third Law

If it doesn't flow, there's more to know.

Learn to recognize all forms of strain—whether at work, in your creative efforts, or in your relationships— as being *unnecessary*. The friction you feel mounting when busy at some labor is never caused by the task at hand, but by what you don't *yet know* about it. This means the only real reason for your strain is that you've got hold of a wrong idea you don't yet see as wrong. This new insight allows you to release yourself by showing you what you need to know. Flowing follows your *new knowing*.

The Fourth Law

Don't take the easy way.

There's no getting away from what you don't know, which is why any time you feel compelled to go around a problem by taking the easy way, that problem always comes round again. And isn't that what makes life seem so hard? Learn to see the "easy way" as a lying thought that keeps you tied up and doing hard time. Getting something *over* is not the same as having it *completed*. And as this insight grows, so will your understanding that the whole idea of the "hard way" has always been just a lying thought as well. Now you know: *the complete way is the easy way.* So volunteer to make the "hard way" *your* way and learn the *real* easy way.

The Fifth Law

On the other side of the resistance is the flow.

There are often times when it feels as though you can't go any farther in your work or studies. But you can learn to go beyond any blockage. Make the following clear to yourself. Those moments—when it feels as though you're least able to get beyond yourself—*are not* telling you that you've gone as far as you can go, but only reveal that *you've reached as far as you know*—for *now*. This higher self knowledge about your true inner position allows you to see the resistance you're feeling for what it really is: a *threshold*, and not a closed door. Walk through it. Nothing can stop you. On the other side of the resistance is the flow. Learning to go beyond *you* is the same as entering into the new.

The Sixth Law

Watch for the opportunity to learn something new.

Everything is changing all the time. That means life is an endless occasion for learning something new. But this means more than meets the eye. Just as you're a part of everything, everything is a part of you. The whole of life is connected. And your ability to learn is part of the wonder of this complete, but ever-changing, whole. Learning serves as a window, not only into the complex world you see around you, but through it you may also look into the you that's busy looking into the world. And when you've learned there's no end to what you can see about the amazing worlds spinning both around *and* within you, you'll also know there's no end to you. So stay awake. Learn something new every day. You'll love how that makes you feel about yourself.

The Seventh Law

Learn to see conclusions as limitations.

If you approach the possibilities of learning about your life as being limitless, which they are, then it follows that any conclusion you reach about yourself has to be an unseen limitation. Why? Because there's always more to see. For instance, let yourself see that all *conclusions are illusions* when it comes to the security they promise. There may be security in a prison, but there are also no choices behind its confining walls. Learn to see all conclusions about yourself as invisible cells. For that's what they are. The seeming security these conclusions offer are a poor substitute for the real security of knowing that who you really are is always free to be something higher.

The Eighth Law

Have no fear of being afraid.

Fear can't learn, which is why you must learn about fear if you ever wish to be a fearless learner. So, the first thing you must learn is how to get past your fear of being afraid. Here's how. The next time a fear of some kind tries to fill one of your moments, try to see the difference between the *fact* of your situation and your *feelings* about it. This is the right use of your mind. For instance, it's a fact that interest rates change. It's *not* a fact you have to get scared when they do. That fear is *not* a fact of life, but only becomes one for you as long as you insist that life perform according to what you think are your best interests. As you learn to see that these fearful feelings don't belong *to you*, but only to *your wrong thinking*, you cease to be afraid, even of your own fears.

The Ninth Law

Never accept defeat.

As long as it's possible to learn, you need never feel tied down by any past defeat in your life. Here's the real fact: nothing can prevent the inwardly self educating man or woman from succeeding in life. And here's why: *wisdom always triumphs* over adversity. But to win real wisdom calls you to join in a special kind of struggle. And if this battle had a banner under which to rally, here's what would be written upon that higher call to arms: "But I can find out!" Yes, you *can* learn the facts. You may not know the real reasons why you feel so lonely or worried at times, but *you can find out*. And you may not understand how you could have been so blind to that evil person's real intentions, but *you can find out*. Take these four words that are freedom's battle cry. Use them to defeat what's defeating you.

The Tenth Law

Learn to let go of painful pretense.

Most people approach their troubles with one of these two non-solutions: they either pretend their problem isn't a problem, or they pretend they've solved their troubles with temporary cover-ups. But their pain remains. It doesn't have to be this way for you. You can learn to let go of painful pretense. Here's how. When facing an old problem, what you *don't* want is another "new way" to *deal with it*. What you really want is to *learn something new* about the true nature of what has a hold on you. To go far, start near. When faced with any pain, *let go of what you think you know*. Act towards your trouble as if you don't know anything about it. This new solution is the only true one because the truth is you *don't know* what the *real* problem is. Otherwise you wouldn't still have it. Letting go of what you think you know puts you in the right place for learning what you need to know.

The Eleventh Law

Persistence always prevails.

If you'll persist with your sincere wish for higher learning, you can't help but succeed. *Persistence always prevails* because part of its power is to hold you in place until either the world lines up with your wish or you see that your wish is out of line. But, for whichever way it turns in that moment, you've won something that only persistence can pay. See the following: if you get what you think you have to have to be happy and you're still not satisfied, then you've learned *what you don't want*. Now you can go on to higher things. And should you learn you've been wearing yourself out with useless wishes, then this discovery allows you to turn your energies in a new direction: *self liberation*.

And now our time will be well spent in exploring yet another kind of learning, a higher schooling that instructs the mind with the energy of the heart. We must always remember that law without love, is like a guide without eyes.

A WISE AND WINNING WAY TO LOOK
AT YOUR LIFE

There's an ancient truth tale about a young man who yearned to study with a renowned master of archery. It was widely spoken that this teacher had achieved perfection of mind. His skill with the longbow was reported as second to none. Admittance to this master's school presupposed a potential student was already advanced enough to strike the small center of a target from a great distance.

But it seems the young student at the center of our story had never even owned a bow before. And so, when his time at the line came to shoot his one arrow— and through trial win admittance to this select school— he failed to hit the mark. He was politely sent away.

The young man's spirits sank. He knew his family didn't have enough money to buy him a bow. How could he practice his art? How would he ever learn the skills he so desperately wanted to understand?

Disappointed and feeling rejected, he returned to his mountain home where, late one sleepless evening, he was struck with an unusual idea. He immediately set out to carve a lifelike statue of the teacher who had sent him away. He delved into his work, paying strict attention to every detail of his archery master's perfected shape and form with the bow. Slowly a strikingly real and lifelike image emerged.

Of course, all the villager's thought his actions strange. Some even laughed out loud at his foolishness. But he didn't care. His heart knew what he had to do. And he was listening only to its instruction.

For the next nine months the young student sat before his completed statue of the master. He studied every detail of exactly how the master stood, of where his one hand held the bow and from where the other drew the string, of the spot where the arrow shaft lay up against the bow, and of where the teacher's fingers dressed the arrow itself. From the arch of this statue's wooden back to the gentle tilt of its wood-hewn head, not a single feature escaped the student's eager eyes.

And when at last the time came around again for the young man to draw his arrow in competition for a place in the master's school, all the other prospective students started again to tease him. They all knew he had yet to own a bow. How could he hope to win?

But this time, when the young man let his arrow fly, it flew straight to the heart of the target. He surpassed them all, and won his place in the school.

But how did this miracle come to pass? The tale of truth that isn't told in the story, but written between its lines, is a higher lesson in learning from the Free Mind.

In the months that followed, leading up to the day of his triumph at the archery contest, this successful student spent all of his time not only studying every aspect of his carefully carved teacher's statue, but in learning something about his teacher that no amount of study could ever teach. Every day, with only his heart as his guide, he would try and somehow look at the world through the eyes of his wooden mentor; so, that in some unknown way, he might learn to see what his master could see at the moment of letting an arrow fly.

And on competition day, because of his unthinkable efforts, the young student hit the mark. In his devotion to his master's art, he came to possess his master's skill, and was rewarded the prize that no one thought he could win.

If we're to win the prize of self liberation, to know the unrestricted life that's light years beyond the world of our ordinary thinking, we too are called to take an unthinkable action.

Before we can enter, and live in, the higher realm of the Free Mind, we must learn to see our life through *its* eyes. Like the young archer in our truth tale, we must first give ourselves to the higher view of the Free Mind, and *then* we'll receive its powers of perfect perception. We must *act* in order to *receive*. If this idea sounds familiar, it should. And, as we're about to discover, nothing is more rewarding—or practical—than this new kind of vision.

Let's look at how meeting life and its events through the eyes of the Free Mind might differ from the way we now see it through the eyes of the me mind.

LEAVE THE "VICTIM LEVEL" OF LIFE BEHIND YOU

When faced with any pain or grief—past, present, or promised—the first thing the me mind asks is: "What's to be done? Who can I speak to about it? What's the best way for me to handle it? Is there any way out?" And at the heart of these complaints, whether detected or not, is the me mind's favorite question: "Why does everything happen to *me*?"

But at the root of each of these fearful questions which seem to seek a way out of the sorrow *lies a secret assumption*, one that keeps us defeated and going around in sad circles. And the deception in this assumption of the me mind is so habitual that if it weren't for the existence of the Free Mind, and its higher powers of perception, this subtle betrayal would be complete. What is this unconscious assumption that almost none can see?

The me mind always begins with the assumption that whatever your current pain may be, it must be real. And, more importantly, hidden in this same unsuspected assumption, is the me mind's wrong reasoning that since that ache is lodged in your heart—it must follow that that pain *belongs to you*.

Even if you doubt the existence of a higher, happier life level, the following is beyond all doubt: *living from a mind that automatically assumes suffering is real, gives you no choice other than to remain a perpetual victim*. This defeated inner condition is the same as being sentenced to a life of perpetual sadness and resentment. Our lives aren't meant to be spent in this wasteful way. Following is a new and much higher way to look at, and solve, this very old problem.

The next time any sadness, or worry of any kind, calls for you, slow the whole of yourself down and work to quietly observe yourself.

Your voluntary state of conscious, but alert relaxation, will stand in sharp contrast to the rapid-fire contents of your own mind as one thought after another races through it, competing for your attention.

Use your consciousness of this contrast, and the higher self awareness this inner conflict naturally creates, to keep you wide awake to these invading thoughts and feelings. This sustained and elevated awareness is vital to your success. Here's why.

No matter how familiar that grief or anger may seem as it floods through you, allow your new awareness to help you just consciously brush aside *what you think you know about it*. Make it your heartfelt intention to *see what that pain is trying to tell you about you*. Here's the explanation.

The me mind knows if it can get you to believe in its conflict and suffering, then *the reasons for that suffering must be real*. This is where the darkness triumphs. In so many unspoken words—words whispered in the dimly lit portions of your own mind—it tells you: "Since this pain is real, your problem has to be real as well."

Yes, there may be a real problem. But it's rarely, if ever, *what we think it is* which is why our long-awaited victory never comes. It can't. We've yet to encounter the real enemy. Get ready.

THE HAPPINESS OF DROPPING PAINFUL DEMANDS

The Free Mind knows the real cause of our unhappiness has nothing to do with which way events or relationships turn. Even though it often feels like it, dark inner states aren't born in the actual unfolding of any present moment, but are born afterwards, from unconscious resistance to any event that somehow opposes the wishes of the me mind.

So, the Free Mind sees clearly that the source of our suffering isn't that life *fails* to live up to our expectations, but that *we live from a nature that meets life with countless unconscious demands*. And contrary to what the me mind would have us believe, happiness is not having our demands met.

Lasting contentment is being free of our own undeveloped and demanding nature. The Free Mind is able to see that the only thing that makes us unhappy *is our ideas about how to make ourselves happy*. The me mind can't see this contradiction in consciousness because its nature *is* this contradiction.

Begin today, right this moment, to see your life through the eyes of the Free Mind. Use its wise eyes to assist you in seeing all the ways in which the me mind wants you to make sense of suffering. *And then see that suffering never makes any sense!*

Meet as many moments as you can with this new wisdom. Look at all of life, and all of its demanding relationships, from the undemanding eyes of the Free

Mind. In this way, if you do your part, you can't help but hit the higher mark. One day the new freedoms you're sure to see, *you will be*.

For one extra profitable inner practice, look for the me mind telling you to run from the pain. For instance, maybe a tormenting thought tells you not to speak up in a meeting for fear of looking stupid. *Speak up anyway!* Allowing *any* pain to tell you who you are—or what you should do in order to avoid pain—is stupidity.

Use the higher vision of the Free Mind to see that the pain the me mind would have you flee, *it* first created—by telling you how to stay safe. The Free Mind invites you to get reckless with what's been wrecking you. Learn to see the deception in any assumption that wants you to believe that there is no higher alternative to your suffering than to endure it.

Never listen to any pain that is asking you what to do about it. The moment you seek a solution to its tormented question, *you're under its authority, which makes you its victim*.

To achieve each new level of happiness, and the higher freedom that comes with it, takes special inner effort. These ten insights, along with a powerful exercise for putting them into action, will help you gain the strength you need to reach a higher, happier life level.

1. Your new life begins the moment you choose to leave your old one behind you.

2. In each moment that you don't choose in favor of your own freedom, a choice was made for you in favor of increased captivity.

3. Without your relaxed awareness of some thought or feeling as it courses through your psychic system, you don't have the choice whether or not *to be* that thought or feeling.

4. You can wake up right in the middle of any thought that may be terrorizing you and see that's all *it was*: a thought.

5. The greatest darkness in the world becomes powerless, and then disappears, in the light of higher learning.

6. Persist with your studies of the Free Mind because within its world, *everything you learn, you earn*.

7. In life, you always become what you love.

8. Learn to look twice at any painful situation and see if what you saw the first time wasn't what the me mind wanted you to see.

9. Any psychological suffering your mind tells you is something you'll just have to live with is coming to you from a part of your lower nature that's killing you.

10. Work consciously, persistently, defiantly to see life through the eyes of the Free Mind.

THE SECRET OF RELEASE AND RELAX

When the doctor taps your knee and it suddenly jerks, you don't get upset with your leg for jumping out of control. Why? Because in that moment, you realize your temporary jumpy experience is an *involuntary physical reaction*.

But, how do you view your emotional reactions when they start jerking you around? Not only are they hard on you, but once they're done, you're then hard on yourself with a negative reaction to your first reaction.

Here's how to release and relax yourself from these runaway self wrecking reactions.

To begin with, understand that you are not your own reactions, anymore than the burst of a flashing skyrocket is the night sky it temporarily illuminates. And yet, it really does feel that way. Let's find out why.

Painful reactions to life events are just *mechanical*, emotional knee jerks. They only become more than a package from the past when the me mind says "I" to the first reaction. This misplaced identification may feel like you, but it's not. And now you can learn this rescuing fact for yourself.

Each time you feel a reaction about to take you over, *just relax from yourself*. Let that reaction be there, within you, *without your involvement*. Don't say "I" to it.

This conscious new action releases the reaction to complete *its* life, instead of stealing yours. It soon fades and you're free. So, relax. And release yourself.

CHAPTER 5

Wake Up To A Fearless New World Within You

WHEN WE SLEEP AT NIGHT, THERE'S LITTLE CHOICE WHEN nightmares come but to let these unwanted forces locked within our unconscious mind run their course. We awaken when we can no longer bear the dream, when it's simply too painful to remain asleep. Once our eyes are open, there's great relief in discovering they'd only been closed, and that our problems aren't real after all. We'd just been locked in the dark theater of our own mind without knowing it. Once awakened, and conscious of our true condition outside the scary scenes within, our fears vanish by themselves. That's what it means to *wake up*. That's part of its sweetness.

Even after we come to ourselves, another more distant sensing spills into the pleasure of our newly awakened self awareness, a nagging feeling we can't shake. Could we still be asleep? Our intuition here is true.

This unusual idea about men and women walking around in a state of psychic slumber is by no means new. From Christ to Khrisnamurti, Plato to Thoreau and Emerson, these important messengers of the Higher Life have all been saying the same thing down through the ages: Wake up man! Wake up woman!

But permit me to anticipate your question. "Wake up from what? And to what?" To help shed light on these important questions, give your full attention to the revealing questions and answers that follow.

"I have moments that seem like lifetimes when it feels as though I'm caught in a bad dream and just can't wake up. The only problem is my eyes *are open* and I'm *wide awake*! What's going on? Is there really a way to wake up and gain release from my own waking life?"

Yes, there is. And we've all known those scary moments of wishing we could wake up from the nightmare of our own lives. But, just as quickly as it occurs to us that we might be in some unsuspected state of psychic sleep, we slip right back into a deep spiritual slumber, and so forget our realization of that moment.

"But why fall back to sleep? That doesn't make sense, especially if it just means going through another bad dream. What can we do to stay awake?"

First, we must understand our real inner condition. In spite of what the me mind would have us believe, only one or two parts of our nature, out of hundreds, have any interest in staying awake. The rest of us is only comfortable when we're sleeping! And these thoughts and feelings are not going to help us disturb their nap! So, our first step toward rousing ourselves into an awakened life, begins with realizing just how asleep we really are.

"Why is that the first step?"

Because this healthy discovery awakens our need to awaken. The highly revered Eastern philosopher Lao Tse told his disciples their chief problem was they were "living in a dream, while not knowing they were dreaming." How do you awaken someone who's in a dream but that doesn't suspect anything's wrong?

"Yes, that's what I want to know!"

Start that person wondering: *if* he or she is really as awake as he or she thinks, then why is his or her life still such a dark and scary place?

"I know exactly what you mean. Lately it seems more and more that the part of my life that's the dream is when I'm feeling at ease, and that it's the recurring frustrations and disappointments that are real. And I know I'm not the only one who feels this way. That's why the idea of relief just doesn't interest me anymore. I want out of this! Is there a way to wake up? *Really* wake up?"

FREE YOURSELF FROM THE SECRET CONFLICT IN SELF CONTROL

Realizing the fresh life of the Free Mind *begins* with the conscious release of your ordinary mind, the me mind.

This higher form of letting yourself go occurs naturally as you awaken to the obvious limitations of living from this lesser self. This process is a bit like one day realizing your favorite old coat is so worn that it no longer keeps you warm. Sure, you love it. But, it's useless now other than as a memory of more pleasant days. You have to let it go.

"This idea of letting go makes sense to me, especially the way you've described it. But how do I do it?"

The internal process of self separation occurs naturally as we become increasingly aware of all the invisible contradictions within our own thinking. Here's just one small example, out of thousands, that can help serve our study.

At some point in each of our lives, we've all seen, or most likely been, that angry person who lashes out at a loved one for not caring as much about something as we *think* he or she should. We measure his or her perceived thoughtlessness against our perfected mental picture of what we *think* it means to care. But *not a single one* of our own thoughts can see how careless—or unloving—we've just been to ourselves, let alone to that significant other. Seeing this contradiction in our own sleeping mind, with all of its wrongful self righteousness, *is* the same as awakening to the dawning of an inner world without it. It's our new self seeing that serves as the alarm clock we need to wake up and to stay that way.

"I've heard about certain other techniques and disciplines that are supposed to help a person stay awake. What about these controls?"

Trying to dominate our destructive thoughts and feelings, or seeking to liberate our "better" parts through some form of self discipline, is secretly at the expense of our freedom, and not in its cause. Freedom from the ties that bind, victory over our own nature, is not a conquest in the usual sense. Try to see the following as deeply as possible: *anything that has to be kept in check must also keep its checker in chains.* The person with this kind of control over him or herself is like an ignited rocket tethered to the ground. The opposing forces eventually cause an explosion. We need release from ourselves, not a better way to live in prison. Keeping these points in mind helps us to arrive at this totally new consideration: what we really need is *distance* from our own highly reactive thoughts and feelings.

"That's a very unusual idea. Although there are times when the thought of getting away from myself does sound appealing. Struggling with the me mind now seems senseless, especially if all we can hope for is new struggles. But how do we create the needed inner distance you mentioned? Is there a special secret to stepping back from myself?"

Start by collecting all the facts you can about your true inner condition. Support your findings with further personal investigation. These actions bring higher discoveries which will inspire you to reach higher on the next round of self study. For a start, the following is an exercise in how to work successfully at self separation.

You can wake yourself up just as many times as you're willing to catch yourself in daydreams where you're the star. This amazing discovery proves that the *only* power the me mind has to keep you slumbering is how much you enjoy feeling like you're in the spotlight on center stage. But you can have something much higher than these bittersweet temporary sensations.

Each time you find yourself daydreaming, give yourself this healthy jolt. Cancel all remaining performances of that show. They're probably just reruns anyway. Your choice to come wide awake, and to live without your dream self is the same as choosing in favor of the Free Mind—the permanent home of your Real Self. This conscious act places you directly in the healing spotlight of the present moment.

CLEAR UP THE SOURCE OF ALL PAINFUL CONFUSION

Imagine going outside and picking up your morning newspaper. But, as you scan the front page, nothing you see makes sense! One headline contradicts another and all of the feature stories run together without a single article reaching any clear conclusion. Your frustration mounts as you struggle to grasp what's happening in your world.

So you turn to the financial news hoping for smoother sailing. No luck! What you see just confuses you more. The business section is filled with comic book characters giving reports on the economy. You knew things were bad, but this is too much! What does it all mean? You can feel your heart beating faster.

Suddenly a rescuing thought comes to mind. Maybe things aren't as they appear. So you call the newspaper, trusting that somewhere in all of the confusion there's a suitable explanation.

Much to your relief, the kind but flustered man on the other end of the line reports that the papers computer software had malfunctioned. All the news run off the press that morning was printed topsy-turvy. After he apologizes for the obvious inconvenience, he says an accurate newspaper will be delivered later that day. The case of the confusing newspaper is closed. All is well in your world once again.

But real life rarely enjoys such tidy endings as the mystery stories we read. Resolution of our confusion comes only about as often as do rain showers in full sunlight. Disorder is more the rule of the day. The briefest glance shows why.

Just like the puzzling newspaper that made no sense because it came off the presses wrong, our own thoughts and feelings often report such contradictory stories it's impossible to tell what's real and what's not. Uncertainty then gives way to fear. And in the search that follows to find some secure conclusion to our mounting confusion, we find ourselves tied to anxious thoughts that only run us ragged, forever hinting there's a sound reason for their rambling, but never getting to it.

It even seems our emotions are a part of this conspiracy to confuse. What could be more mind-boggling than to *know* you feel one way towards someone or something and, within the space of a single heartbeat, suddenly find yourself feeling just the opposite?

Whenever this internal turn-around happens, all we really know for sure is we don't have a clue! Was it love, or *is* it hatred we feel? And then these same doubts throw us right back into the same old mental mill again.

Doesn't this scenario sound awfully familiar? It should. For the masses of mixed up human beings this is their only way of life: an endless struggle to make sense out of what makes no sense to begin with. But, for anyone tired of running him or herself through this daily grind in the mind, it's possible to cancel all of this confusion forever.

A DAY IN THE WEIRD LIFE OF THE ME MIND

The me mind lives in a constant state of confusion and conflict, because it believes the world *it imagines* is the only world there is. The problems associated with this mistaken point of view should be obvious, but here's just a small glimpse of the tremendous pressure this false nature has to endure to live in such deep imagination.

Picture how difficult your life would be if you'd been hypnotized into believing that there was no such thing as gravity. Everywhere you went, you'd always be explaining to yourself, and others, why things weren't weightless and floating around!

Think of it! Every stationary object would frighten you. And to keep things in the air where, according to your hypnotized mind, they're supposed to be, you'd always be trying to juggle one more thing. Worse yet, you'd resent anyone who tried to tell you that water flows downhill, even though you can see it does. Sounds like a tough way to go through your days, doesn't it? And yet, this is exactly what a day in the life of the me mind is like.

Reality for this nuisance nature is a sliding scale that's in endless motion to accommodate the countless contradictions between the real world and its imagined one. And when it can no longer maintain its superimposed order of life, because of some massive collision with the real one, this unenlightened mind just finds a way to write the story all over again. Whatever form the unexpected, or unpleasant, event may have assumed, the me mind just reconfigures it—until it assumes a pleasing shape that blends into the landscape of its imagined world. This endless cycle of collision—followed by reconstruction—is how the me mind convinces itself that all is in order and under control.

Vernon Howard helps illustrate this unnatural psychological sequencing with the following example. Picture an archer who first shoots his arrow into the air, and who then goes and draws a bulls eye around where the arrow has landed! This is classic me mind mechanics at work. By cleverly rearranging reality, according to its conditioned need for the moment, this unconscious nature believes it has control. But it doesn't. Confusion and fear rule this life level where the me mind is king.

CALL ON THE PROTECTIVE PRESENCE OF THE FREE MIND

The Free Mind is never confused or out of control. Its Cosmic Order can't be turned upside-down by unexpected events, anymore than daylight is confused by the onset of nightfall. Why? Because the nature of this Supreme Self and the flow of life's events are *one*. This special wholeness empowers the Free Mind to *know* what's a natural part of itself and what is not; it *knows* what belongs to it and what doesn't. The truth of this celestial fact is more easily understood by turning our attention to an example common to us all.

Each of us can effortlessly identify what's "our own." When it comes to personal possessions or ideas, we just know what's originally ours. It's not necessary to think about whether or not something belongs to us.

This same ability holds true for the Free Mind, only at a higher level. Its timeless intelligence detects anything not a part of its own pure essence. This Higher Order *does exist*. And while the evidence of its presence is subtle, it's not beyond our perception if we know where to look.

For instance, most people don't know much about the mechanics of music, but they can still recognize a bad note if a musician happens to hit one. There's a part of almost everyone that *knows* when a note is out of place. In short, we may not understand the complex nature of musical harmony, but *there is something within each of us that instantly recognizes what is not harmonious*.

This tells us that harmony—the expression of perfect musical order—*is already* present somewhere within us. But this important discovery heralds the possibility of an even greater potential: a world within us that is completely free of confusion and conflict. Further investigation will show us how this higher life level is available to us and only waiting to be realized.

Whenever we walk into a room where people are angry or anxious, even if the dominating negative state is invisible at the moment, we can still detect its unpleasant edge in the atmosphere. The unnatural discord, along with its punishing presence, is both sensed and refused by the higher order within us.

But this effortless form of spiritual safety only occurs as long as we can "hear" that silent part of our own Higher Nature, the Free Mind. It knows, *which becomes our knowing*, that the negative vibrations in the room are not a part of itself. *This awareness is our protection*, because as long as we remain aware of the discord as being apart from ourselves, we don't fall to the level of the people around us. This is good for us, and it also provides a healthy shock for anyone else in the room conscious enough to notice that we're not taking part in the darkness. Our awareness lights theirs. Now they have a chance to change.

PUT YOUR LIFE IN PERFECT ORDER

The Free Mind is a perfect warning system for detecting and, with your cooperation, rejecting any and all psychic intruders. Its uncommon Intelligence never complies with the presence, or demands, of any fearful negative state.

On the other hand, the me mind is forever trying to make sense out of suffering. It finds relief by creating new ways to put old pains into a different order. This unconscious activity is what the me mind calls clearing up the confusion!

But the me mind can't clear up the confusion. How can it? *The me mind is the source of it.* How can this lower nature ever determine that sorrow is one of the ties that bind as long as it holds onto sadness as an important part of itself? Fear, doubt, and anger are also included in the painful order of the me mind, so how can it ever find freedom from negative states? *It can't. But you can be free of it.* Here's a good beginning.

Make a list of the things in your life that you know—or sense—are out of order. Start by writing out a few of the more common negative thoughts and feelings that may still be a source of personal confusion for you.

For example, you may already know that jealousy, impatience, and laziness are three self compromising states that don't belong in the order of your life. As a helpful guide, you may want to follow the format I've developed for this inner exercise.

1. Angry thoughts telling me to hurt others because they've hurt me *are not a part of the order of my life*. **No anger belongs to me.**

2. Frightened feelings towards another person *are not a part of the order of my life*. **No fear belongs to me.**

3. Nervous trembling over an uncertain future *are not a part of the order of my life*. **No trembling belongs to me.**

4. Confusion and doubt in the face of unexpected changes *are not a part of the order of my life*. **No anxiety belongs to me.**

Learn to see through and let go of those parts of yourself that think it unimportant to shed light on any of these out-of-order inner states. Daring to boldly illuminate them is the same as lighting your own way. Your conscious cooperation with this new inner light is the same as inviting the Free Mind to place these confusing states in their True Order *for you*.

The gifted Swiss philosopher Henri Amiel explored the Free Mind. Of its perfect powers for creating inner harmony he wrote: "The being who has attained Harmony, and every being may attain it, has found his place in the order of the Universe, and represents divine thought as clearly as a flower or a solar system.

"Harmony seeks nothing outside of itself. It is what it ought to be; it is the expression of right, order, and truth; it is greater than time, and represents eternity."

FREEDOM FROM THE FEAR OF LONELINESS

No fear belongs in your life. This doesn't mean that you walk out into the street without looking, or that you close your eyes to the dangers lurking in people or dark places. But it does mean that if your walk through life hasn't been an inwardly fearless one, you don't have to take one more frightened step. There's no doubt in my mind this is true. And you can be just as certain.

Everything depends upon what you really want. Want to shake off the shakes once and for all? Then begin by getting fed up with the shaking, which means to stop doing what the shaking tells you to do. You wouldn't ask a ghost to show you the way out of the house it haunts, so why take directions from any fear on the way to end your trembling?

Starting right now, tell whatever it is that frightens you to go rattle its chains someplace else. Maybe you're afraid of being left alone? Would you be surprised to learn that you may not know what real aloneness is all about? And further, that if you'd dare your fears to leave you alone, you would never have to feel lonely again? Yes, it's true.

Loneliness is not a fact of life anymore than war is the beginning of peace. Loneliness is an effect of fear. And when you're free of fear, you have no fear of being alone. Follow the logic by the numbers and then prove it to yourself:

1. Loneliness is first a fear, before it turns into a painful longing.

2. Without the fear, there is no longing.

3. When the ache of the longing disappears, so does the feeling of being lonely.

Ridding yourself of fear is the same as losing your loneliness. So go ahead and choose to lose both. Yes, you can do it. You can consciously change the kind of inner company you keep any time you want, provided you're willing to take a stand in favor of your own Higher Nature. Your refusal to ever again fear person or circumstance is a great start.

Perhaps you're thinking, "But how do I overcome what comes over me without a warning?"

Again, just refuse to be afraid. But, if you think this conscious rejection of fear means you have to be brave or strong, it doesn't. The Free Mind never asks you to do—or to be—anything beyond the scope of your present understanding. And yet, you are charged with one definite responsibility.

In order to spill its courageous nature into your life, the Free Mind asks that you don't fall back on old and weak excuses when you falter in your quest to be fearless. So you said "yes" once again, because you feared to say "no." Or maybe you promised yourself, "never again," and before the words were out of your mouth, you were off and running, acting out the same old cycle of self defeating behavior. Listen to what the Free Mind says about being a flop: "So what! Just pick yourself up and start all over again!"

It may not feel like it, but conscious trembling and tripping over yourself are early stages in your ultimate victory over fear. Even though it may be temporarily hard on you, don't accept any of your own excuses for these necessary missteps.

1. Refuse to blame the way the world turns for your own anxious or desperate actions.

2. Never again justify a choice made by yourself against yourself, such as fawning over another for some imagined advantage.

3. Disavow any thoughts or feelings compelling you to explain why you're in the right when you know you're really wrong.

Enough said? Good. Then no more excuses!

Why take such a tough tactic with *ourselves* when our stand is against *fear*? To begin with, it helps to see that any excuse we make to cover up a fearful action is just the secret seed of another fear. And who wants to plant a field of fears? Besides, it should also be clear that only another fear looks for a good reason to be afraid!

But there's a much deeper spiritual reason for voluntarily strengthening our resolve to be fully fearless. Following are two surprising, but perfectly true statements. Give each your close consideration.

1. The more determined you can become to live without fear, the clearer it will be to you just how frightened you really are.

No doubt you're shaking your head and wondering: "Why would anyone want to know the depths of his or her own fear? What could possibly be the profit in this kind of self discovery?" These questions set the stage for our surprising second lesson.

2. Just as the love of freedom that courses through our veins could never live under the tyranny of any dictatorship, so does the Free Mind refuse to tolerate the presence of any fear that enslaves the Spirit.

BE STRONGER THAN ANY INNER BULLY

The fall of fear begins with our heightened awareness of fear's presence. Out of this higher level of self conscious-ness comes something as mysterious as it is grand: *the spiritual intolerance of fear*. This deep, unnegotiable dis-dain for fear comes to us in advance of the powers we need to win our freedom from it. And the arrival of this supreme strength—that ultimately leads to lasting self liberation—is one of the great mysteries surrounding the Free Mind. The following story illustrates the victori-ous powers we invoke when we take a stand against fear.

I once saw a great western movie where a good sheriff had given up on the people of his frontier town. They were cowards. Not a one would take a stand against a band of evil-hearted bullies that had cor-rupted the whole territory. Frightened and defeated by events that seemed beyond his powers, the sheriff took to the bottle to hide from his own fears. Life was miser-able. There was no peace for anyone.

Also living in this same troubled town was a quiet stranger—a man who didn't even own a gun, let alone know how to use one. But came a fateful day when, despite his deep and moral hatred of confrontation, he knew he could no longer hide. His life had become intolerable. It was painfully clear there was no living with himself if that meant he'd have to live the rest of his days in terror.

And so, even though he couldn't get either the sheriff or the townspeople to stand with him, he called the bad men out into the street for a showdown. The next few scenes of this film were just tremendous. Let's review them to see what secret insights they hold, and how they can help us win our own showdown with fear.

Just as it looked as though this hapless and help-less stranger was about to be cruelly gunned down to the ground, the unbelievable took place. All of a sudden, from all around him, shots rang out. A rain of bullets poured into the gang of murderous thugs. The quiet stranger was saved. And what about the bad men? Defeated once and for all in this showdown at high noon, it was the end of their reign of terror. But, what happened? How had good been empowered to win the day? Here's the story behind the scenes.

Rallied by the courage of the stranger in the face of impossible odds, the sheriff and townspeople were moved to a change of heart. And when they came to his rescue, they gave him the powers he didn't have himself, but that he needed to win his struggle with evil. A happy ending to be sure. But this inspiring story from the days of the old west also reveals how the Free Mind can run any bullying fear out of your life.

When you can no longer bear being pushed around by fears that never leave you alone, challenge them to show themselves to you. Call them out into the light, just like the quiet stranger did at high noon. Never mind if this makes you tremble. Those, and any other shakes, will be vanquished along with the rest of the inner villains by the friendly, but all powerful forces of the Free Mind.

Your conscious refusal to accept fear as a part of your life invokes the Free Mind to stand with you. And in this showdown, the outcome of the battle was long ago decided. Fear has lost. You win. The Free Mind invites you to experience this victory for yourself.

Starting to think differently towards your own fears is the same as learning to act differently towards them. Use these ten truths to help you begin thinking fearlessly. Higher actions will follow.

1. When you find that one part of yourself that wants freedom from fear more than it wants *the freedom fear promises*, you've found the real beginning of the end of fear.

2. An awakened consciousness never fears losing control because it never gives itself away.

3. Self awakening starts with catching yourself having been spiritually sound asleep.

4. Let go of any fearful inner state by shaking yourself awake from the self created dream that produced it.

5. The one thing that really puts the scare into what's been frightening you is your conscious decision to be no one.

6. Nothing in your life can be any more complete than *you* are.

7. Your awareness of any fearful disturbance must precede your freedom from it; this is the one True Order upon which self rescue is founded.

8. No punishing thought or lonely feeling belongs to you, so start seeing their presence as the unreal, rude intrusion that they are.

9. Don't be afraid to tell anything that's frightening you to get out of your life.

10. Waking up to the power of the Free Mind is the same as waking up to all that you are *intended to be*.

Break Into Your Day And Watch It Go In A New Way

You don't have to *believe* that there's a fearless world above your present mind. You can live within its perfect order any time you choose. Make this choice for your own freedom starting right now.

Practice breaking thought. Go mentally silent. Just become aware of yourself without thinking about it. Break into that swarm of thoughts and feelings, over and over again, with *your awareness* of their presence. This will silence them *and* show you where you have been.

This important practice of conscious awareness allows you to *know in each moment* that there is *you and* your thinking, *you and* your emotions. *All* are present *at the same time*. This knowledge brings choice.

Consciously breaking thought—becoming aware of your Self within the existing order and values those same thoughts unconsciously impose—helps you experience the liberating difference between being a captive of your own mental machinery and being in charge of it.

Come awake to yourself as often as possible. Break into your own thinking with your awareness of it. Break thought ten times a day, then a hundred times, and keep going. Watch how this powerful practice establishes a New Order in your life free of all conflict and confusion.

CHAPTER **6**

The Secret Of Owning
Your Own Life

T HERE IS ONE HEARTACHE WE KNOW ALL TOO WELL. AND
each time it makes its unscheduled, unwelcome
appearance it becomes that much clearer we've
never really lived without the presence of this grief. It's
that familiar to us. But, as quickly as this disturbance in
our being can appear, it vanishes again, which leads us
to believe that either we've overcome this feeling, or
that it's passed. But we're wrong on both accounts.

Who is this dark visitor with both a permanent
passkey to our inner home, and the power to punish us
at will? *Our never-ending need to feel approved.*

There are few places in our life where this pressing
want to be wanted doesn't compromise our true best
self interests. And believe me, almost none are exempt.

From the person who longs to be like someone else
whose exterior manner of polished confidence he or
she thinks commands approval, to that person whom
he or she envies, who secretly spends all of his or her
energies to appear confident in order to win that same

approval; *neither one* knows the peace he or she is either seeking, or pretends to possess.

Our increasing insight into this fundamental fact about the barrenness of the unawakened human nature is an essential ingredient in our search for freedom. Within this seldom perceived secret lies the necessary, but shocking, realization that no man or woman has what he or she really wants.

BE STRONGER THAN THE APPROVAL SEEKING SELF

In my book *The Secret Of Letting Go*, I tell the story of Alexis, a bright, young executive with her sights on the top of the ladder of a giant global corporation.

One evening Alexis gets the shock of her life at a VIP business party. She accidentally discovers that not a single one of her superiors, all the way to the top of the ranks, has any real power to help her achieve her dreams. Alexis learns all at once that the fulfillment she longs for, *she will have to find within herself*, or not find at all.

But, as temporarily disheartening as these revelations are for Alexis, it's the events of that evening which finally awaken her, and so place her, on the road to owning her own life. She was able to see, as we must now see for ourselves, there was neither any person with the powers she imagined him or her to have, nor was there any *real* need for her to be powerful in the way she'd always believed.

It's time to snap ourselves out of the painful delusion that any individual either possesses or, in some way, can grant us the power we need to possess ourselves. Let's gather the facts that will lead to our inner liberation.

No man or woman is powerful of him or herself. I know this. You can too. What we've always mistaken for power in another is only the overpowering false belief that someone else holds the keys to our happiness.

No one else holds the keys to your life. As this awakening dawns within you, your new understanding will also reveal a brand-new view of the world around you.

People you once thought of as powerful will be seen as weary pretenders *who need you* to complete their charade! What a wonderful, liberating surprise! And from the seed of this special insight flowers the first of many new inner strengths. Let's take a personal and up-close look at three of these new powers and the insights that empower them.

1. The Power Of Self Command

Casual courage develops naturally as it becomes clear to you that the people you've always looked to for help can't really help themselves. Now you know there's no advantage in giving yourself away to others or to their empty promises.

2. The Power Of Relief

Once it's totally clear no one else can do for you what only you can do for yourself, you no longer have to live with the anxious fear that someone you were counting on may let you down.

3. The Power Of Relaxed Confidence

Since you know there's no real advantage in gaining the attention of the world around you, you can relax when around others who are always engaged in tense competition for it.

No one can give us the approval we seek, because it isn't his or hers to give. And the more we understand the truth of this higher fact, the less inclined we'll be to give ourselves away.

Seeking and receiving approval from others is like sitting down hungry to an imaginary meal. You're invited to eat all you want, but no matter how much imaginary food is served, you can never get your fill. Your hunger remains. No fictional feast ever satisfies.

But this fact isn't so apparent when it comes to our appetite for approval. We still look to others for our sense of self even though *the very moment it's received, it must be renewed.*

Believing we can't be happy without the approval of others is like thinking that we can't see beauty without someone else's eyes!

Time and time again, we come to the same spiritual lesson: no one can give us that which can only be found within our Self. But we must transform our sensing of this timeless Truth into our personal understanding of it. We must do the needed inner work, which alone leads to owning our own lives.

The following question and answer dialogue is a condensed version of many conversations I've had over the years with sincere seekers of self liberation. Permit its insights to provide you with the principles and powers you'll need to become your own person.

MAKE THE FEAR OF BEING "NO ONE" FADE AWAY

"I know it's a mistake looking to someone else for a sense of myself. I really do. But what I don't understand is why this need for approval runs so deep and so strong. I've heard lots of theories, but what I'd really like now is some insight into how I can keep from giving myself away?"

Before we can clear away the invisible obstacles blocking our path to self possession, we must first understand their *real nature*. An honest admission of our present condition gives us an excellent place to start. We seek the approval of others because as long as we think someone else feels good about us, it allows us to feel that way about ourselves as well.

"Well, what could be wrong with that?"

It may help if we look at this confusing condition from a slightly different angle. Let's see if the way in which we look at ourselves through the eyes of another still sounds as pleasing after we place our new perspective into the form of a probing question: *What good is any feeling we may have about ourselves, if it only lasts as long as others agree to it?*

"Yes, I see what you mean. There's certainly a lot more to this issue of seeking approval than meets the eye. What else do I need to know to set myself free?"

Looking for ourselves in the eyes of others throws us behind the walls of a psychic prison. The door slams shut each time we find ourselves feeling good about ourselves simply because someone has given us a needed nod of approval. Let's investigate this strange sequence of psychological events that leaves us in a prison of our own making.

Whenever someone approves of us, it gives us a feeling we like. These silent emotions tell us that we're good, wanted, or in some way important. But the real pleasure in these sensations is that it secretly serves to strengthen the way *we want to feel about ourselves*, that we're worth being cared about, and that our existence has meaning.

"But what's wrong with those feelings?"

If these positive emotions were the true end of a happy story, there wouldn't be a problem. But they're never the end. *At the same satisfying moment* of our being unconsciously identified with this feeling of being approved, something else is happening to us deep within our own uninvestigated nature.

As our approval-provided feeling of self worth starts to fade, *which all such feelings do*, we begin feeling *as though we too are about to fade away!* But, if we could only see behind these feelings of fading back into obscurity, what we'd see is that our feelings of self worth aren't really disappearing at all. *They're only going through a state of flux, a psychic transformation that turns these once-pleasing emotions into their own undesirable opposites.*

Now, the same feelings that had confirmed us only moments before become a source of misgiving, internally questioning us as to our own importance. So we start to worry. Maybe we're no longer needed? Maybe no one loves us? And as this vicious, invisible, psychological process moves towards its inevitable conclusion, *we begin feeling a subtle form of fear*, a distant dread.

We've all felt that unpleasant inner pressure of a brewing anxiety. It heralds the coming of insecurity and self doubt, in much the same way as distant thunder warns of an approaching storm. And the stirring of this first dark wave within carries an unspoken message on its winds. It warns us of a serious loss of some kind if we don't do something right away to shore ourselves up.

"How true! And so we go out looking for approval all over again! No wonder we never break free from this approval seeking business. But what can we do? Is there no way out?"

Yes, there is a way. You must act on our new knowledge.

"What do you mean? What should I do?"

Your new actions won't be so much what you do as *what you don't do.* Here's the bottom line drawn out for you in three points, followed by an important summary which also includes a special instruction and encouragement.

1. Never again go looking to another human being for his or her approval.

2. Never again fawn over anyone to show that you're on his or her side.

3. Never again exchange your smile in the hope that someone who is capable of betraying you, won't.

Summary and Instruction: Face your fear of disappearing, *without doing anything about it* ... and something *will* disappear. *But it won't be you.*

The only thing that will fade from view will be your own fear of fading. And, as it disappears, what appears in its place, right before your inner eyes, will be the *you you've been looking for* in all the wrong places!

This is the real beginning of having your own life, of being your own person. Only this time your sense of yourself is coming to you from *reality* itself. And *this* is the only approval you'll ever need, the *only* one that *never* fades.

"There's still one thing I'm not sure about. How can it be wrong to want or enjoy the approval and respect of my peers?"

Winning approval and respect from others and wanting it have very little in common. When we're willing to go the extra mile—*to be* or *to do* what is *true*, especially if there's a personal cost attached to it—others see our sacrifice and their approval is a spontaneous reaction to seeing excellence in action. Enjoyment of this kind of approval is both natural and non-binding.

But, if our initial wish is to attract attention or applause, then we're doing what we're doing for all the wrong reasons. Then we have neither good works, nor respect. Approval may be awarded, but *never sought*. The approval we seek makes us debtors of our own fearful feelings—and of whomever makes us temporarily forget these fears.

Use these ten facts to help free yourself from the cycle of seeking approval. Your studies will start you on the road to being your own person. You will succeed!

1. Trying to build a life on feelings given to you by others is like thinking you can sail from Alaska to Hawaii in a boat made of ice.

2. Make all empty feelings reveal their real contents to you.

3. You can submit to painful situations, or you can study them out of existence.

4. Only the higher awareness of the Free Mind, which *sees* all feelings are fleeting, doesn't fear their fading.

5. The approval of a hundred thousand people still can't make you feel *real*.

6. Even in those moments of feeling completely isolated, you are never alone in the way the me mind wants you to believe that you are.

7. Our chief shortcoming when self sinking feelings make their bid for our attention is that, instead of becoming conscious of their presence, we become their unconscious captives.

8. Seeking a sense of self permanence in the way others regard you is like trying to make a plaster cast of the wind.

9. The feeling of being apart from life is only the effect of being lost in a crowd of thoughts and feelings that are telling you who you are.

10. When you stop looking for yourself, and start *seeing* yourself, you'll find what you've been seeking all along.

COUNT ON FULL SELF COMMAND WITH THE FREE MIND

There are countless worlds spinning both within and around you every moment of your life. These worlds and all of their forces are invisible to the usual mind. But, whether perceived or not, their unseen influences actually determine whether your walk through life will be a pleasant or punishing one.

What few have ever understood, but which you can, is that you can choose which of these worlds you live in.

But, before we can make these obviously crucial choices that determine the quality of our lives, we must *first know what these choices are*. And to be able to know what our real choices are, we must be able to *see* them. This unique ability to be able to look into our own inner universe, and to consciously choose the life we want from within all of its myriad worlds, is one of the special powers of the Free Mind.

The higher freedom, to choose our life experience, always sparks special interest in our regular class discussions. In these meetings, students find it valuable to look at troublesome, or challenging real-life situations, and then consider how they can be made trouble-free by the presence of the Free Mind.

So, for the sake of this study in conscious self command, let's create an imaginary coffee shop and fill it

with people during a busy lunch hour. The two principle characters in this illustration are Bill and Sandra.
And although neither knows the other, both are seated
at the same lunch counter having their meal. Now we'll
add one more vital ingredient to our story, and then
we'll go on with the illustration.

Bill lives from *the me mind*. Sandra sees her world
from *the Free Mind*. Let's see what happens next.

Suddenly, off to the left, comes a loud, crashing
sound that almost makes Bill jump right into his soup
bowl. His head whips around, angry at the uninvited
intrusion into his thoughts and the pleasure of his food.

At the same moment, Sandra comes instantly alert
to the possibility of any danger. When she sees there's
no real threat to her safety, she consciously releases
her body's natural physical tension.

In less than another moment, Bill locates the area
of the disturbance. He sees the busboy has dropped a
tray full of dishes. And to make matters worse, now the
coffee shop manager is yelling at the hapless boy.

A heartbeat later Bill begins feeling very uncomfortable with the developing situation. He doesn't catch
the image that leaps up and lodges in his mind. The
cafe manager's angry red face and high, harsh tones
remind him of his little league coach that he still
resents from his youth! His thoughts lash out at both
the manager before him and his boyhood manager of
days long gone by.

Sandra, while not turning to watch the quarrel,
feels a flush of discomfort go through her at the sound
of conflict. But just as quickly she dismisses its presence. She understands that this unfortunate incident
has nothing to do with her.

By now, Bill wants to get out of the coffee shop as
fast as he can. He wants to get away from all of the
unpleasantness he believes is being thrust upon him.

So he gets up to go to the cashier. But, in his preoccupation and his hurry, he doesn't see that the check for his meal has already been placed on the counter next to his plate.

Sandra finishes her meal too. Out of the corner of her eye, she notices Bill racing over to get into line to pay for his food. She catches that his tense actions have made her a little anxious. So, she deliberately slows herself down and double-checks her seating area to be sure she's left nothing there. Then, picking up her check, she heads over to the cash register and gets into the line.

When Bill finally gets up to the cashier, the smiling lady behind the counter asks him for his check. Realizing that he'd forgotten it in his haste to make a quick exit, Bill assures her that he never got one. She politely assures him that he did. Her gentle correction both embarrasses and angers Bill. He pivots on his heels and walks indignantly over to his seat. Finding the check there as he was told he would, Bill starts muttering to himself—half out loud—about the rudeness of the employees and the poor service he'd received.

In the meantime, Sandra watches the person in front of her, and behind Bill, getting increasingly disturbed over Bill's delay in paying his tab. She steps back slightly from this person—and from her own reaction to his increasing levels of agitation. By this time, everyone in line is now uneasy and on edge. That is, everyone but Sandra.

At last Bill is able to leave the scene. Still stewing and brewing over the event—even as he walks away from it—he wonders silently to himself why the world has to be such an unfriendly and out-of-control place.

Sandra pays her check, counts her change, and leaves a small gratuity for the service. Later that afternoon, she returns home to spend a quiet, contented evening. Her comfort comes to her from the knowledge that, living from the Free Mind, she's in charge of her own world.

Please don't think this study in the difference between the me mind and the Free Mind to be in the least bit exaggerated. Like Sandra, you too can learn to live from the comfort and control of the Free Mind. Or, you can be like poor Bill, who commands nothing other than the delusion that he's in control of his own life. Let's see what else we can learn from our lunchtime illustration.

THE AMAZING DIFFERENCE BETWEEN THE ME MIND AND THE FREE MIND

It should be clear that even though Bill and Sandra were in the same physical world of the coffee shop—at the same time and under the exact same exterior circumstances—inwardly they were really living in two completely different universes.

Bill's universe is a place beset upon by other worlds that seem to crash into his at will. Chaos follows. Sandra's universe doesn't wobble.

What Bill calls choice is really only his explanations for his reactions. Any action born out of an unconscious reaction can't be called choice, anymore than a billiard ball can say it chooses its direction in the opening break of a pool game. Damage control is *not* the same as free will.

The problem is that Bill has yet to discover that the only worlds with which he collides *are all of his own making*. If he had this higher vision, he would have no crashes with life, no painful encounters of any kind. Like Sandra has learned to do through her liberating relationship with the Free Mind, he could *choose to step out of the way* of what's been wrecking him.

But, Bill can learn. He can start with the small but powerful intention to want to learn all about what he has called his own world. His wish to learn is the power he needs to rise above himself. And from this new and superior inner vantage point, he'll see that he isn't the one, unified world he's always imagined himself to be, but that he is really many worlds, most of which know nothing about the existence of each other, even after they collide. His shocking discovery about the fragmented world he calls himself marks the real beginning of a new life for him in a new world. You can learn how to live there too.

Anyone willing to become conscious of the real differences between these two disparate life levels, can make the journey from the me mind to the Free Mind. A careful review of the following section will help heighten your awareness of just how great these differences can be. Take all the time you need to make the contrast clear between these two possible levels of consciousness.

1. The me mind always asks: "What's going to happen to me?"

    The **Free Mind** *sees* this question is born out of fear, and the **Free Mind** knows better than to scare itself.

2. The me mind always asks: "What else can I do to be free?"

    The **Free Mind** understands that real freedom is never an *exchange* for this or that—because if freedom *depends* on anything, it isn't really free at all.

3. The me mind always asks: "Why did he or she do this to *me*?"

   The **Free Mind** knows that no one can cause you to suffer without your unconscious consent.

4. The me mind always asks: "What's the use in trying?"

   The **Free Mind** realizes that the only thing useless about any troubled time is those nagging, negative thoughts that want you to see life through their eyes.

5. The me mind always asks: "What can I do about what happened to me?"

   The **Free Mind** knows the real basis of a problem doesn't exist in what *has passed*, but is within what you're permitting to happen to you in the present moment.

6. The me mind always asks: "How can I avoid that scary situation?"

   The **Free Mind** sees that the suffering you fear will come *is* the very pain you fear.

7. The me mind always asks: "In what way can I cover up my mistake?"

   The **Free Mind** understands that hiding any mistake is the same as chaining yourself to your own wrong thinking, which only guarantees you'll make the same mistake again.

8. The me mind always asks: "Wouldn't I be happier someplace other than where I am?"

The **Free Mind** knows that a divided mind is *always in conflict* and that *conflict doesn't know anything about being happy.*

9. The me mind always asks: "How can I win the approval of others?"

    The **Free Mind** questions the reality of any feeling that only lasts as long as others agree to it.

10. The me mind always asks: "What do I need now so I can stop worrying?"

    The **Free Mind** understands that real self security is the natural expression of a quiet mind.

CHOOSE IN FAVOR OF YOUR OWN FREEDOM

After you've closely considered these ten contrasting mental conditions, create your own list using similar guidelines. This is valuable inner work to do for yourself. The clearer it becomes for you that there's a choice available between living *with* the me mind or *from* the Free Mind, the easier those choices are to make, and the happier you'll be. Choose the Free Mind. Choose in favor of owning your own life.

New and conscious self command begins with learning to think toward yourself in these new and higher ways. Here are ten additional ideas with which to start changing your view of you.

1. Your real life is *not* a fixed condition, anymore than a river is a concrete road.

2. In life we're either self commanding or *we are being commanded.*

3. Don't see individuals as powerful; see them as either being at peace with themselves—or *under some other power*.

4. *Fear of the unfamiliar* is the me mind's attempt to turn that moment of encountering something brand-new *into one it can recognize*.

5. Whenever meeting what may be new to you, dare to look at it with a sense of wonder, and watch how the fears disappear.

6. Whatever freedom's path requires of you it will also supply you, if you just keep walking.

7. Reactions don't know anything about relief.

8. As you increasingly realize that your life contains *much more* than your present experience of it, this awareness helps create conscious expectation which, in turn, leaves room for something *new* to appear to you.

9. Learning all about the mechanical nature of your reactions is the same as knowing what to do about them.

10. The happy day will come when you *know* that if you have *one* problem, you have one too many.

THE ONE POWER GREATER THAN ANY INNER DISTURBANCE

The Free Mind wants you to have its power of perfect self command. You need only know the right way to ask for its silent strength and you'll be the ruler of your own day. Begin asking now with this higher action and watch how strong new results follow.

The next time you feel as though you just have to talk to someone about something that's making you uncomfortable or unhappy, *don't do it*. You can learn to use that pressure to free yourself from all such feelings that want to push you around. Here's the explanation: *finding relief is not the same as finding strength*.

That disturbance within you, whatever its reactionary nature, isn't real. It's *really nothing* that just *feels* like you. That's why you mustn't do what it urges you to do, or you'll unconsciously lay claim to *its* weak and self compromising nature.

From this moment forward, consciously challenge the right of any dark disturbance to direct your life. Stand your inner ground until its demands drain away. Negative states have no real life of their own, so consciously withdrawing your life from theirs is the same as commanding their dark presence to fade. Once the pressure is off, you can then choose to say something, or not, about the conflict that was in question because, at this point, you'll be in command of yourself *and* the situation, instead of being unconsciously commanded by it.

CHAPTER 7

Connect Yourself To A Life Of No Self Compromise

A S OUR INSIGHT INTO OUR OWN HIGHER NATURE CONtinues to grow, so does the depth of our certainty we've stumbled onto an uncompromised source of strength and wisdom. But it's the discovery behind our breakthrough that promises to finally reveal the treasure we've been seeking.

Little by little it dawns on us the source of all these higher self possibilities is founded within our being. It's our own essence that dwells uncompromised. And as the emerging presence of our True Nature, the Free Mind, makes itself increasingly evident to the mental and emotional worlds *within us*, the confusing worlds that spin *around* us also begin to make much more sense.

Those seemingly ancient fears of feeling abandoned start to fall away by themselves. And that weary wish of ours to know for sure there's an order to things slowly transforms itself into the clear-cut confidence that, not only is there a plan in place, but we can actually enter its perfect symmetry. The possibility of a personal, yet fully harmonized independence becomes our reality.

Our new eyes show us that everything, including ourselves, lives under Higher Laws. Every day, in countless ways, we see where the Celestial expresses itself in the common.

And in our newly awakening knowledge, that even the simplest truths are but a reflection of a still greater power, our hearts are instilled with new daring. We become willing to risk more because we fear less. And we're less and less frightened because now we know, beyond the shadow of any doubt, that if these higher principles are coming down to us from somewhere, then these same Laws must lead back to whence they came. This discovery is the same as having found the way back home.

ATTRACT POSITIVE LIFE RESULTS WITH THIS POWERFUL SECRET PRINCIPLE

"I must admit I get excited hearing ideas such as these. But, more often than not, my excitement turns to agitation. It's like being handed a travel brochure, a boarding pass, and then somehow missing the information where my plane is leaving from! Much as I want to, I can't seem to get off the ground and into the air. I need something more solid to go on. What can you tell me that will help me put some real wind beneath my wings?"

Do you remember the opening lyric to the classic song "Love and Marriage?" If not, allow me to refresh your memory: "Love and marriage go together like a horse and carriage."

Along with its memorable melody, this particular song has endured the test of time because hidden in the heart of its simple lyric is a celestial law about the power of attraction. If you recall, the rest of the lyric goes on to say: "This I'll tell you brother, you can't have one without the other." This innocent line, "you can't have one without the other," expresses, in earthly terms, a powerful cosmic principle we can use to help us reach the Free Mind.

"Really? What principle is that?"

The law of attraction. We've all heard similar ideas before that express this same principle in different terms. Remember the tried and true sayings "birds of a feather flock together" and "like attracts like?" This lyric, "you can't have one without the other," tells us that everything, from feathered creatures to heavenly forces, has a specific essence that draws to it those elements that are like itself. Can you see the truth of this?

"Yes, but what's the value of knowing about these laws of attraction, or any other higher principle, unless they can connect me with the Free Mind? How do I put the law of attraction into practice in my everyday life, in order to realize the celestial one?"

Let's begin with a common emotional or mental quality that you find particularly valuable. Choose any one you please.

"Alright then. How about clarity? In my work, as an account supervisor, being clear is essential to the overall well-being of my company's operations."

Good. Clarity is one of my personal favorites. It's vital in everything we do. Now, when you think about the importance of being clear in your communications or choices, what are some of the positive benefits you've received, either as a result of being personally clear on some issue or from someone else being clear with you?

"Where there's clarity I find increased efficiency, and that translates into greater productivity. There's also a decisiveness I find when things are clear."

Right. And aren't there other constructive traits and characteristics to be found in the presence of clarity? How about confidence, purpose, and casualness?

"Yes, there are. And I'm beginning to see what you mean. The one attracts the other."

We can, and *must*, be more definite about our findings. *We can't have one without the other.* Which means further that just as all forms of clarity are connected to a certain calmness, so is the opposite of clarity connected to constant conflict. Can you have a casual, confident manner about yourself in an important meeting if you're unclear as to why you're there? Or would you be nervous and on edge the whole time?

"I've been in that uncomfortable position before, and I didn't like it one bit. But, I know we're not speaking of individual moments such as these, rather how to change what attracts them to us in the first place. Is that correct?"

I think you've said it well. If we can see, in fact, how positive inner states lead to positive life experiences, then we can also see that negative inner states *must* attract negative results. Shedding light on this dark cycle will help us see into a totally unsuspected source of self compromise.

ONE QUESTION CANCELS ALL SELF COMPROMISE

Whenever things are confused in our mind or heart, we'll also find within us hesitancy, doubt, and fear.

Taking the law of attraction through a simple progression reveals that once we're in the hands of one of these shaky inner states that consort with confusion—such as anxiety—what else can we hope to attract but other attending negative states—such as tension and irritability? These brusque emotions are brothers to impatience, whose sister is intolerance, which gives birth to cruelty and hatred.

Our new knowledge is indisputable. It shows us that we can only expect darkness if we cloak ourselves in shadows. The lesson is clear: one attracts the other because, in reality, *one is the other*. Fire doesn't attract smoke. Smoldering is to burning what anger is to hatred and violence. Which brings us to the principal point of our study.

There can be *no* compromise, *none*, with any conflict or negative state within ourselves. We must resolve to never again go along with, or agree to, any mental or emotional state of negativity. And should you ever hear the me mind trying to convince you that such true self command is impossible, it's within your power to make this dark inner imp, and all of its dark forecasting, disappear. Just quietly demand that it answer one of *your* questions *before* you accept *its* terms of defeat. Ask it this: What's going to happen to me if I *continue to cave in, or make compromises*, with what has been compromising me?

The me mind has to avoid this question at all costs. It knows instinctively that if it ever gave you the real answer, it would mean the complete disappearance of any doubts you may have as to what you must do to be free of self compromise.

"I've never seen this so clearly before, but it frightens me as well. I don't think I'm strong enough to end what I suspect is just the tip of a dark, inner iceberg."

We must not fear our findings. Nor must we worry whether or not we're a match for what weakens us. I know these wary emotions *feel* like they're on our side, because of their *seemingly* protective nature, but again, *you can't have one without the other*. Forget what these habitual thoughts and feelings are telling you. Listen instead to what the Free Mind wants you to hear. Fear and worry—no matter what they may be about—*always betray the one they possess*. Besides, throwing these inner troublemakers out of your life for good is not your responsibility.

"Now I'm confused. I thought you said we shouldn't compromise with any self darkness. If we don't liberate ourselves, then who or what will?"

There must be no compromise, but we must stop thinking in terms of overpowering what may be standing over us. The only real solutions are those which have the power to lift us above the world of our worries. *Letting go of any conflict is really just growing beyond the need for it.* This is why our sole responsibility is to be willing to stand in the right inner place. Only there can the higher laws of attraction do for us what we've been unable to do for ourselves: separate who we really are— the Free Mind—from what we are not—the me mind.

THE SECRET OF TAKING THE NEXT STEP HIGHER

Imagine a bustling train station with multiple embarking gates located all on one large platform. From this one elevated stand in the middle of the station there are lots of trains departing for the scorching deserts, as well as one that goes directly to a cool mountain resort.

Getting on the right train for the pleasures of the high country depends upon knowing from which gate that one special train departs. And we can only put ourselves on the right track—in that place of authentic self lifting power—each time we refuse to harbor any self defeating state. Why? Because our new resolution to remain awake and *not* be self compromising is clearly the right action. And it's this correct inner stance towards our unwanted psychic intruders that connects us with both the possibility—*and* the power— for us to take the next step higher.

Let's look at how we can apply what we're learning about these laws of attraction to some of the commonly occurring events in today's hectic life.

Suppose someone walks into your office and drops the bomb that your company has unannounced plans to lay off several employees, and that no one knows who these unfortunates are going to be.

Without these higher principles to meet this unexpected moment, the fear would surely take control of you and the moment. In no time, you would be the victim of your own self compromising plans for revenge on an insensitive company, or some such enemy.

Of course, at first glance, feeling scared and getting angry in an event like this seems like it makes sense. But a closer look clearly shows how it betrays.

We can't have fear without anxiety. Anxiety can't exist without unconsciously comparing what we hoped would happen, to our new fears that it won't. And connected to this spreading fear our expectations won't be realized is our growing resentment of the situation, or person, we blame for wiping out our hoped-for happiness. So bitterness spreads. And as it does, it whispers to us that since we've already lost our future, why should we do anything more, for anyone, in the present? Now defiance has the reins, and in no time, self righteous anger courses through our veins. Let's stop here for a moment.

Wouldn't you say this description is a pretty accurate psychological profile of someone who hears such potentially bad news in his or her work place?

"Yes. I'd say you've described it very well. But I never realized before that these negative states were so interdependent and interlocking."

It's impossible to have one sad or sour state without another. But there's still much for us to see. Negativity, like all forms of thought, is actually physical in nature. All things physical, *all* forms of matter, have mass. And any mass in motion has *momentum*. Now, with these facts in mind, let's go back go back into our illustrative story and see what the momentum of this negative state has to ultimately attract.

So now the boss walks into your office—or you see him at lunch—and he asks you to do some extra work. But with the feeling of being betrayed still fresh in your heart, you can't help but meet him and his request with a full-blown negative state. The impression you make on him is indelible.

Later on, at a time unknown to you, this same superior starts to review who he's going to keep on and who to let go. And he chooses to release you. Why? Because among other items weighted in his decision process, he recalls your barely masked aggression and obvious resistance to his request. Do we need to take this illustration further, or has the point reached home?"

"Yes, it has. But what's the alternative?"

"We can turn the tables on these troubles by employing what we've learned about the power of attraction. So, let's start the story over and put ourselves in the place of this formerly self punishing person. In our new scenario we receive the same bad news. But this time, the first thing we do—instead of falling into fear—*is become aware of it* as it tries to pull us down. Why this action? Because *we know we can't have one fear without another*. We work very hard to stay inwardly awake to its punishing presence in our psychic system.

"But that doesn't make the fear go away!"

HAVE NO FEAR OF DOING NOTHING ABOUT ANY FEAR

We mustn't try to *make* this negative inner-state—or our situation within it—*do* anything. The me mind always wants to do something with fear. But what we want is to be *free* of fear, not find something new to do with it! This is why we must do nothing but remain right there, aware of our fears and worries, *but doing nothing about them*. Never mind what the me mind wants us to consider as solutions to our sinking situation. Going inwardly alert, but silent, is all that's really within our power—*at the moment*. Any other action would be fear's. And we already know what happens to us when we assume this mistaken psychological position. That's not the way for us any more. We want something higher.

"Higher, yes, but how do we get there? How do we take ourselves out of the tough spot we're in?"

By *not* letting anxiety or worry dictate the terms of our future actions, we take the only step we can that's *clearly* not a part of the fear we feel. In a way, it could be said that we take the right step by *not taking the wrong one*. The *real* point here, and we must experience the miracle of it for ourselves, is that *the next step will come*.

Our success in separating ourselves from the forces that compromise us is as much under law as are the ones that have always left us in the lurch. Everything we need for this new inner success must reveal itself if we'll just wait for its arrival. The Free Mind always fulfills its promise if we cooperate with the wisdom of its ways. Now let's return once more to our psychological story and see how our new understanding attracts a new and brighter outcome.

So there we are, facing the bad news—but also resolutely facing our fears at the same time. Since we now know there's really nothing else we can do at the moment that isn't on fear's terms, we just go back to our business as usual. We do our work. Only now we're active *outwardly and inwardly.*

We listen neither to the clamoring of those around us—about the impending doom—nor do we heed the shouts from our own mind hammering our inner ears. If we do this, to the best of our ability, one of two things *has to occur.* And both results are excellent. Both are success.

Now when we run into the boss or he asks us to do some work—above and beyond our usual job—we just *do it.* No complaints. No resentment. We're not going to do *that* to ourselves anymore. We know better than to be bitter! And the boss notices our effort to *be* the right kind of person. It's natural that he's attracted to the rightness in our attitude.

And when that crucial time arrives for personnel evaluation, to see who stays and who goes, we get the nod to stay. Why? Because our new attitude won for us what we had feared to lose.

And even if this part of the story doesn't happen in quite the way it's been written, we've still won a major victory. Why? Because any time we turn our backs on what frightens us, we also turn our backs on the self compromising acts those fear-filled conditions attract. Instead, in the absence of fear and self compromise, we attract what is fearless, which is the same as saying we attract the next higher level of life.

Review these ten points to help attract the powers you'll need to reach the Free Mind.

1. Release your natural need to be *free.*

2. The feeling that you must somehow prove yourself is a lie you no longer need.

3. The right way to ask for more from life is not to increase your demands, but to release them.

4. The clearer you resolve that you'll no longer accept suffering as necessary, the sooner it will stop.

5. We can only be as strong as we are wise about the ways of weakness.

6. Use every disappointment to show you that you need never feel that way again.

7. *All* negative emotions are self limiting.

8. Self correction is the seed of self certainty.

9. Knowing that you attract what *you are*, helps you want to be different.

10. The power of a Free Mind puts *every* wind at your back.

NEW ANSWERS THAT BRING A NEW LIFE

Picture a man who just heard that one of his closest friends has betrayed him. How does he respond? What's his first answer to this ordeal?

Anger that includes plans for revenge.

Imagine a woman who suddenly realizes she's going to be late for an important appointment. There's no way to make it on time. How does she meet the pressure of this moment? What's her first answer to running out of time?

Anxiety that includes inventing excuses she hopes will be believed.

These are different people under different circumstances, but they've made the same miscalculation.

They both have the wrong answer. To understand their error, let's take a closer look at how each arrived at his or her mistaken solution.

The man who found out he'd been betrayed thinks his anger is a source of strength. And he also believes his heated plans for making the score even will make him feel better. But anger is never real strength, and revenge is always self wrecking long before it ever touches its intended victim. What this man doesn't see is that the reason his heart aches *isn't* because of what someone has done to him, but because of what he's doing to himself by embracing punishing, raging thoughts. He can't see the real reason he aches is because *it's his own answer that's hurting him.*

The woman who's late for her date is certain her anxious feelings and worried thoughts can help her find a way out of her predicament. What she doesn't understand is that her feeling of being squeezed into a tight spot is because she's temporarily tucked away in a darkened corner of her own mind. What she can't see is the pressure she feels *isn't* because she's late, but because she keeps jumping headlong into a torrent of cascading emotions. She doesn't understand that the crushing rushing she feels *is a part of her own answer.*

Summary: *Your answer* to the challenge of any moment—and *what you experience as the quality of your life* in that moment—*are one and the same thing.* In other words, *the way* you answer life's events, and what you experience *as your life*, are really *one.* Let's examine how this works.

If your answer to some sad memory that floats through your mind is to just drift along with it, why should you be surprised when you suddenly find yourself being carried over the falls of deep grief? The reason you have the feeling of falling is because *you and your answer are never apart.*

You can't separate yourself from what you receive from life any more than the ocean is apart from its own waves.

Within the space of each beat of your heart, you get the exact measure of the answer you gave to life the moment before. No more, no less: Life is always true in this way. Without fail, and without judgement, life speaks directly to you through your own immediate experience of it. Learn to listen for its wise council whenever you meet a moment. What it always says is: "Here is *you* back".

The Free Mind knows that reality is a perfect mirror. It always reflects exactly what's in it. But the me mind forever distorts everything it sees in order to justify its concealed, unconscious intentions. This is why we must always be willing to meet life from this higher Free Mind. It alone is the perfect teacher because this fearless nature never denies what it sees. And your life can be just as light-filled and light-hearted as is this pure, elevated Self, *if* you're willing to see that when there's something sour in your life, it's *your answer* that's bitter.

How To Choose The Right Answer For Any Wrong Feeling

Don't be afraid to see that most of the answers you presently meet life with are the wrong ones.

... *Self doubt, anger, denial, anxiety, aggression, worry, resentment, ambitiousness, envy, greed, self righteousness, sarcasm, one-upmanship, demands, cynicism, avoidance, recrimination, dependency, expectations, coercion: all are wrong answers that can only supply secret aches.*

You may be wondering, "Well then, what's the right answer for me? How can I be sure of making the true choice? Or even if there is such a thing?"

That's easy! Here's why. Do you remember in your school days, during exams, there were some questions that came with multiple choice answers? And how there were always those times when you were able to come up with the right answers—not because you knew them—but simply because *you knew that none of the other answers offered could be correct.* In other words, *you arrived at what was right by knowing what was wrong!* You may not have known it then, but by deliberately eliminating what was false, you were employing an ancient and wise technique to come upon what's true. And contained right within this powerful principle is a truly amazing secret.

Each time you refuse to choose wrong answers to live from, you've just stepped that much closer to coming upon what are new and true answers *for you.* Then, you'll have *their reward:* a quiet mind, a contented heart, and complete confidence.

Regardless of how unpleasant any circumstance seems at the moment, always remember: *it's impossible to answer any situation with negativity without casting yourself into that same self created darkness.*

There is always a higher, happier answer if you'll only learn how to ask for it. Again, this kind of conscious self suspension—of putting your habitual mind and its answers on hold—can *seem* scary at times. But one day it will be your greatest pleasure to realize that you don't need any answers that want you to be afraid.

The more you understand about the Free Mind and the nature of the way it fearlessly answers life, the stronger you become yourself. Use these next ten insights to help you to realize an uncompromising inner strength.

1. Everything under the sun is governed by invisible higher laws.

2. Seeing that the common and the cosmic are connected is the same as knowing you can find your way back to the Free Mind.

3. The laws of attraction are at work everywhere and on everything, from birds of a feather all the way to heavenly forces.

4. Your conscious agreement to *never again* compromise with any negative inner state attracts what you need to be free of that state.

5. Should you ever feel fear over what you see in yourself, calmly recall what happens to the breadth and depth of an iceberg as it drifts into the increasing warmth and light of a brighter sun.

6. Conscious dissatisfaction with your present way of answering life attracts a higher order of answers.

7. Not taking the wrong step is the same as taking the right one, as when you refuse to let anxiety dictate any of your future actions.

8. Rage or resentment is never a good answer, because closer inspection shows it never makes sense to burn the house down to save the barn.

9. When the best answer you have is to get negative, you're better off with no answer at all.

10. Growing into the realization that you never meet anything other than your own nature is the same as growing into your new nature.

REACH THE SAFE HARBOR OF THE FREE MIND

A man once stowed away in a canvas-covered deck-side lifeboat aboard a tramp steamer. Late one night an unexpected storm soaked his only set of clothes. Wet and shivering and without knowing what else to do, he stole into a darkened cabin and grabbed the first uniform he found there. No sooner was he dressed than the steamer hit a reef. And when it lurched, he fell down and hit his head knocking himself unconscious. When he came to his senses, he heard the voices of the crew yelling, "Abandon Ship! Abandon ship!"

Dazed and confused about who and where he was, he looked down at himself in the red glare of the emergency lights and saw he was dressed in a captain's uniform. He came to immediate attention. After all, his mind carefully reasoned, there was no choice. He was the captain! He would just have to go down with the ship. And then, in the next heartbeat he remembered his true identity. He *wasn't* the captain. He was a stowaway on a steamer just trying to make it back home.

What relief! This wasn't his ship. He wouldn't have to go down with it after all!

You need never go down with any thought or feeling that tries to drag you under, no matter what it claims you owe to it.

The next time you notice yourself coming up with some sinking answer to life such as, "I can't" or "what's the use?" Qr "I'll never make it," turn immediately to this uncompromised answer of the Free Mind.

Say silently to yourself—about that painful thought or feeling—"that's not my ship!" Then just step back and *let those thoughts and feelings go down while you stay up.* Consciously separate yourself from all these sinking states and their self compromising nature, and one day you'll sail into the safe harbor of the Free Mind.

CHAPTER 8

Possess The Permanent Safety Of Your True Nature

LOOKING TO YOUR OWN THOUGHTS, FOR SOLUTIONS TO problems created by the way you think, is like jumping on a steamroller, and asking it to ferry you across the ocean.

The message at the heart of this insight, concerning the limitation of thought as a tool for self liberation, is concisely stated by the brilliant psychologist and author Carl Jung. "The greatest and most important problems of life are all, in a sense, insoluble ... They can never be solved, but only outgrown."

In other words, we need to let go of our struggles with what we *think* has us tied down, and invest our vital energies in changing our nature. We must learn to leave behind us, instead of serving, that fictitious self which is forever building, and then falling into, some self created snare. Spiritual education is self emancipation.

Outgrowing the problems—*created in the way we think*—begins with realizing the need to not only understand the nature of these invisible building blocks known as our thoughts, but to be able to peer into the structure of the invisible world these same thoughts create.

Since most of us know very little about the machinations of our own hidden mental realm, we're mostly unaware of how its unseen conclusions keep us serving gods that can never be pleased. Which further explains why our lives are spent—not in naturally outgrowing our problems—but in grovelling before them. With these facts in mind, the following short study deserves our close attention.

Thoughts, regardless of how they may be elaborately grouped together, are still individual elements. Even when our mental attention is completely captivated by what appears to be a horde of horrible things about to run us over, that mindless mob in our mind's eye *is still just one thought*—only calling itself many miseries.

When individual thoughts of a similar nature are collected together into groups, this collection of single thoughts can convey a broader reflection that we call an *idea*. For example, this chapter is presented to you in single sentences, single thoughts, which serve to convey a larger *idea* about the nature of thought.

Each of these ideas, as they either enter into, or are created within the mind, are then sorted into appropriately conforming groups which help the mind to form *concepts*. And it's these concepts—our mental pictures—that have always been spoken of as being worth the proverbial "thousand words."

One additional interesting note: the inner glue, the energies that meld these concepts together, and that blend their often diverse, individual meanings into a more holistic one, comes from our emotional center. It's this emotional quality that gives these mental constructs their vivid coloring and vitality, which seems to endow these psychological pictures with a life of their own.

As should be evident, these marvelous, but largely mechanical, workings of the mind present no problems in and of themselves.

In fact, if our mind were to just play its assigned role, all would be well for us. Order, and its freedom, which is the heart of intelligence, would prevail. But it doesn't. And we're obviously not well. What has happened?

Somehow, and it's really of little or no difference as to when or why, the mind began to look upon its own subjective constructs of thought—which are merely mental representations of reality—*as being the actual reality* they only serve to represent. From being a wondrous creation, the mind began to think of itself as the creator. It moved from being an expression of words into believing that it was the speaker, and it fell in love with the sound of its own voice!

HOW TO WIN NEW SPIRITUAL STRENGTH

If we were to see someone trying to warm himself on a winter's night by snuggling up to a color photo of a fireplace, we would easily recognize this person as being deluded. We know that the glossy paper image which he clings to for life-sustaining heat is powerless to do anything but mock his obviously oblivious mind.

But this unfortunate man can't see the futility of his own misguided actions. Why? Because it's his own mind, his level of consciousness, that has confused a mere *representation of reality for the fact of it*. Mental pictures have no reality other than to that level of consciousness which creates them.

This exaggerated illustration, of a man trying to warm himself with a photo of a fire, hints to us of a common, and yet virtually undetected glitch in our own mental machinery. While you and I may not stand beneath a photo of a waterfall to get cool and wet, *we do try to stand on images.* And no image is permanent or real. Here's further proof.

We live with certain unspoken, but flattering mental pictures of ourselves. For instance, maybe we believe we're strong, the unafraid type. We may even have others in our lives who, because of their image of being too weak, look to us to tell them how to conduct their lives. As long as our self picture of being wise, strong, or kind remains intact, it only makes sense to us that these people are better off trying to mold their lives after ours. But then, as it always does, reality bursts our pleasing self picture. Pop goes our beautiful bubble!

Perhaps a bitter feud that's been long-brewing finally erupts in the home. Or there comes some unexpected bad news at the office. In a flash, we may find ourselves either trembling in the face of some shaky situation or fawning over some person of "power." A person who, coincidentally, we had only moments before been telling off from the safe and secret confines of our now fearful mind. Where did all of our strength go?

1. It was never there!

All we ever possessed right up until the moment of that encounter with truth, with reality, was a pleasing picture of ourselves as being someone strong. Which leads us to:

2. No image *of being self commanding* possesses either the strength or confidence it sees itself as having.

But our discoveries about the hidden nature of our weakness lead us to a surprising conclusion. Here we find the seed of a new strength because we understand at long last:

3. We are never betrayed by life.

Our betrayal is fashioned for us from our uninvestigated beliefs that *what we're given to believe* about ourselves, and about others, is *reality. And it is not.*

We're betrayed by our own present level of mind which is incapable of understanding that *none of its thoughts about a thing is ever that thing those thoughts think of it as being.* For your consideration here's additional, valuable proof of this important insight, as well as how this mental confusion—about what's real and what's not—impacts us on a personal level.

We've all known those trying times when our own loving thoughts suddenly turn into their oppressive opposite of resentment or rage. This regretful shift in our nature occurs when we're confronted with pushy people, or events, that manage to overpower our current image of what it means to be loving.

And while we're on this subject of spirits that suddenly downshift, please note this one other important observation. Our instant transformation, from being caring to outright caustic, only makes sense to us as long as we continue to listen to the me mind explain why this behavior is rational or necessary.

On the other hand, the Free Mind *knows* there's no force in the universe that can push real love into any ugly shape. This Supreme Nature knows love has no opposite. Its only wish for us is that we too come to see all false loves as being false friends who are *never* there in time of need.

One point begs clarification at this juncture. When the images we have of ourselves as being loving collide with the facts that show our pleasing self pictures to be only touched-up phonies, these shocking experiences *are not* the proof that love, or its wondrous healing powers, doesn't exist.

Love is real. And we're never closer to it than when given the chance to see what is unreal about ourselves. Learning to welcome these healing moments—of seeing what is false within us as being false—is the same as welcoming what is true. And, as we'll discover in our continuing studies, a brush with the truth is to touch reality.

The Real Cause Of Feeling Like A Captive

Before we can know the true goodness or power of something, be it the love we long for or the freedom which dwells in the purity of the present moment, we must experience *its world directly*. This inner union, where we move from simply being aware of something wondrous that may be about us, into the conscious realization of that wonder as a part of our own nature, is the heart of the genuine spiritual experience. By entering the Real World beyond thought, we merge with Reality. Let's state this important idea in another way.

We must realize the *truth* of something *before* we can know its power. If it makes this portion of our study easier to grasp, the words truth and reality are totally interchangeable. The truth of anything and the reality of it are one and the same condition.

The following illustration illuminates this last vital insight for you. Be patient with yourself. Wait and see how you already understand more than you give yourself credit for knowing.

In the physical realm, direct contact with the truth of something, with *reality*, is commonplace. In fact, the true pleasures in our daily lives are the spontaneous expression of these healthy meetings with reality. Perhaps you can think of other natural examples you'd like to add to the forthcoming one.

To know the strength of a bright summer sun, you need only go outside and stand in its deeply penetrating rays. In *that* moment, as you drink in the sunshine, the fact of the sun's light and its force unite for you, and you are certain of both. You couldn't waver in your conviction of the sun's warming powers, even if someone were to challenge you about their existence because, having stood in the sunlight, the *Truth* of it has become yours.

But, when it comes to the invisible spiritual kingdom within, the seat of reality itself, our direct contact with the *Truth* of its self liberating powers is far from commonplace. And as long as we remain as we are— strangers to the reality of our own True Nature—we have no choice but to wander through the imaginary world of the me mind, isolated from what is timeless, and denied the pleasure of *knowing* that permanent freedom of individuality which only reality can bestow.

That we're separate from the reality of life, and its full potential, is something almost everyone feels. It may have never occurred to you before, but it is this disquieting feeling of having unfinished business, *of being incomplete*, that's at the heart of our feeling captive.

The freedom we seek from the ties that bind is really a search for our relationship with reality. And, if we're ever to dwell in this higher world, where the fact of freedom—and its power—*are one thing*, we must find a way to enter its timeless domain.

But where do we look for this peaceable realm called reality?

Let the following dialogue, taken from one of my discussion groups, help shed light on any questions you may have about how to make direct contact with the Free Mind.

The Keys To The Kingdom Of
The Present Moment

"I know, or at least deeply sense, the truth of these amazing ideas. But *how* do I come to know the reality of a timeless life? How will I ever arrive at that quiet place within myself when everything about my world remains so hurried and so small?"

Let me pose a riddle to you. Solving it will help you start looking in the right direction for the treasure you desire. What's the one condition within which everyone, everywhere, lives in and shares in common with everything, and all without knowing it? Here's an extra hint. There's an endless world which surrounds you at this very instant that never changes, and yet, is always and forever new.

"I can't imagine. Is there such a kingdom?"

Most certainly. It's called *the present moment*—the focus place of all known creative forces in the universe. We all live within the realm of this timeless domain, but don't see it, much in the same way fish are unaware that the water in which they swim is the life-giving crucible of their existence. For most of us, *the present moment* exists only as a mental concept, an idea we more or less accept about *a time* that is ironically, in reality, actually timeless.

"If there really is a place of such power, where the entire creative forces of the universe come together all at once, what makes you believe this supposed singularity is the present moment? What evidence is there for such a conclusion?"

Let's look into this question together. Is there really anything, anywhere, that *isn't* a part of the present moment? But before you give me your answer, consider that even your memories of the past, as well as your hopes for the future, happen *only* in the here and now. Now, can you see the truth in these initial findings?

"I must admit to never thinking about this before. But clearly, since *it's never not now*, it follows that the present moment has to be at the root—or at least be an acting part of—all that there is."

Alright, let's make this concept even clearer in our minds. Where are *all* energies expressed?

"Yes, I see. You're telling me that the present moment is that one point of life's expression!"

Good! A few more questions and answers and we can rest on this point. When does Life start? And when will it end? When do cause *and* effect take place? Are they really separate forces? And when is it that we meet every challenge? When are problems born, and when are they resolved? When do we feel pain? And when is our healing?

"I think I'm beginning to understand. How extraordinary. Even though my mind has always thought of these individual moments as being separate from one another, they all take place in the *now*. And it's *always now*. Is that correct?"

Yes, but now we must go just a bit deeper. Just relax and allow the next few ideas to reveal their hidden treasures about this timeless kingdom of the present moment.

"My spirit is willing to learn but, to tell you the truth, there are times when I'm not sure if my mind is getting the message!"

Don't be concerned with whether or not your mind is grasping all of these principles. It's helpful to understand spiritual logic, but ultimately, *it's your spirit toward these higher studies that determines your success*. If you'll just remain open to what is new, what is true will take care of the rest.

"That's very encouraging."

Then lets keep going. Our discoveries reveal that the cosmic energies which both form and animate all of life, and the constant unfolding of the present moment, are really one and the same unceasing expression. But, having resolved the truth of this, we must dare question ourselves if our *idea* of this everlasting *now* is the same as knowing the truth of a truly timeless state? Or, is the fact of forever something quite apart from our concept of it? What do you think?

"They're clearly not the same. I think I'm beginning to understand. The truth of something, which is the same as the real experience of it, cannot be found in any idea about it. Is that what you mean?"

Right. So even though a perfectly present moment can be conceptualized, the very thoughts which empower us to imagine this timeless realm are coming to us from the world of *time*. This discovery shows us that *all* concepts, regardless of their nature, *are not a part of the present moment*. Can you see the fact of this?

"Yes, I believe I can. But what do these insights have to do with contacting the Free Mind and winning spiritual freedom?"

Because in the perfectly present moment *there is really no you*. At least not in the way you now conceive of yourself.

"What do you mean? How can you say there's no me? I am me!"

Bring all that we've learned so far in front of you, and then listen to what the Free Mind has to say. You are not the *you* that you *think* you are. All the images you have of yourself, including your memories and future plans—this total identity—is just an intricate, thought-constructed concept mistakenly accepted as being the essential you. This is *not* who you are. You are neither your name, nor any other title the me mind may give you with which to know yourself.

To the degree you're willing to see the truth of this temporarily shocking revelation *about who you are not*, you'll realize, in turn, the power this discovery has *for releasing you from you*. So welcome all of these fascinating and self liberating findings. Dare to ponder them. Within their gradual dawning comes your direct contact with reality. In your hands are the keys to the kingdom of the present moment.

A TALE THAT TELLS OF TRUE MAGIC

Nothing brings higher ideas and spiritual concepts to life in quite the same way as when they're presented to us in stories and parables. Imagine yourself as the central character in this next illustration. Allow the lesson from this truth tale, and the ones that follow it, to show you that any psychological suffering is needless, and how it can be dropped.

It was too quiet. He could feel his skin tightening. Actually, it felt more like he was shrinking, but he knew that was impossible. On the other hand, he knew that if he asked his burning question, it might just be perceived as some kind of irreverent insult, like asking a master mathematician if numbers could be counted on.

But he felt as though he had no choice. The moment had come. And yet, it wasn't bravery that opened his mouth, that brought forth the words he could hear himself speaking. It was the weight of the silence that had finally pushed him over the edge. And, in a faltering voice, the young apprentice spoke. "Please, tell me, Master. Is there really such thing as magic?"

The wizened old man's answer came so quickly, so surely on the heels of his own question that it startled him. "Oh yes, to be sure. Indeed there is."

The apprentice felt better immediately. After all, over the last few days, he'd envisioned the Master turning him into a frog or a bat for even daring to ask such a question. But nothing bad had happened. Nothing at all. And so he asked his next question more resolutely. "Well then, Teacher, just what is real magic?"

Before the sound of his own words had left his ears, the Master had crossed the room and was standing right in front of him, looking deeply into his eyes, as if searching for something. Apparently, whatever it was he'd been looking for he found, because his eyes seemed to suddenly focus on something far away. And in an unwavering voice, the Teacher spoke to him. "Real magic is when you know there's nothing in this world—or within the countless other realms—*that has any power to hurt you.*"

And then, as almost an afterthought, he finished the conversation as he walked across and then out of the room saying, "Oh yes, and real magic isn't something you possess. *It's what you are.* Now, finish your chores and then get back to your studies." And the door closed itself behind him.

You too have a fearless nature that knows it cannot be hurt, defeated, or dominated by anything, an essence that never suffers. But you don't live from it. Your present life, and this source of supreme strength, live in two completely different worlds. Your inner work is about building the bridge of understanding that can take you from who you think you are to the reality of your True Nature. And to go far, we start near.

END THE SECRET INNER WAR CALLED
SELF COMPARISON

As our inner investigation continues to reveal, this present life level of ours is really a secret construct in conflict, a physical expression of the invisible nature of thought. Suffering is both a part of this thought nature and of all the worlds it creates. But this thought nature, our own thought life, no matter how sublime, *is not our real nature*.

The mind that suffers is actually moved to feel that way *because of the way in which it thinks*. You and I hurt, in the way we do, because a feature of living from thought is *to experience its nature as ours*. And suffering is one of the unhappy characteristics of thinking we are our own thoughts because *it's the nature of thought to divide*.

Division is how thought operates. On the practical level, thought is the power that lets us know apples from oranges. And there's no problem there; that is to say, until these same thoughts tell you that your apple is smaller than my orange! And then, out of this comparison, the suffering begins.

Nowhere is this suffering, and the false sense of self it creates, so evident as in the bondage and anguish created through the unconscious act of self comparison. Let's look at an extremely common, but painful form of comparison known to us all: comparing who we *think* we are to who we *think we should be*. This kind of self comparison is nothing but the same as self created conflict.

Maybe you're thinking, "Isn't the drive to improve ourselves natural? How can just thinking about myself and wanting to be better create conflict?"

You tell me. How would you describe someone in a ceaseless war *within himself, about himself*, other than someone who lives in self created conflict? There can never be a winner in any battle when there's only one contestant! Lets see how such an internal war comes to exist in the first place.

Self comparison, and the internalized conflict it naturally breeds, can't exist without the presence of conflicting images and concepts *about yourself within yourself.*

Some of these concepts of self include what you think is good or bad about your character, how you think others perceive you, and what you hope to change about yourself.

But, by far the most devious of these concepts, and in a special sense, parent of them all, is this last great deception: that the "you" who is involved in this constant conflict called self comparison *is different* from everything else within you that's being compared. And it's not.

That "you"—that familiar sense of self that's either satisfied in any given moment, or who's in some kind of torment *over having to be you*—isn't the real you at all! And neither is the false sense of life these incessant sufferings provide *your real life*. The whole painful package created by these unseen works belongs to the me mind. It derives its unlife through the ceaseless mental comparison of *what was to what is*. And then, from this dissatisfied mental platform, envisions a new you in the future that will live punishment free.

But I repeat, *this persecuted nature is not you*. Which means that neither are any of its heartaches, anxieties, and endless fears, a part of who you really are. This true spiritual finding is the foothold by which you can climb to your freedom. However, it's suitably ironic that this same discovery is also one of the most confusing for seekers of self liberation. This question invariably arises. How is it possible, when suffering seems so real, for anyone to say that it isn't? Let's look at this deep concern from one more viewpoint.

The psychological pain you feel is not *your* pain. It's an effect of the inevitable crash that occurs between unconscious concepts you have about yourself and reality. An illustration will help make this point.

Throw a stone into an unobstructed stream and it produces friction. The water has to flow around the stone. Who *you* really are is the stream, *not* the stone. And just as the stream would know, if it were a sentient being, that the friction in its flow doesn't belong to it, but to the presence of the stone within it, so you too can realize that the pain you feel doesn't belong to you, but *to the mistaken concepts you have and hold onto about yourself*. And there's more.

Now imagine this same stone struggling to change the course of the stream, so that its waters flow *the way the stone thinks it ought to!* Sound familiar? Wanting people and events to do as you want them to is the exact same struggle. Now you know why you feel so weary. But this metaphor also provides clear evidence of another possible way to go through your life.

FLOW WITH THE PRESENT MOMENT INTO THE FULLNESS OF THE FREE MIND

Here's an inner life exercise of immeasurable value. Think of these new instructions as a kind of special cleansing agent, *but not* as a way to improve yourself. Let me explain.

When we wash a window, to clean away its obscurities so that we can better see the beautiful outdoors, we haven't improved the nature of the colorful scenery we can now see clearly. All we've done is take away what was preventing us from enjoying what was there all along. This is exactly how the following exercise will work for you. Soon you'll see all suffering as just something that was unnecessarily in your way. Enjoy your new, bright view.

Start by dropping everything that isn't a part of the perfectly present moment. Work consciously at clearing away all those rock-like, hardened thoughts and feelings that aren't a part of what is the naturally occurring, spontaneous *now*. For extra help in discerning what's a part of the present moment and what's not, connect this next insight with all that you've learned in this chapter.

Everything arises within the present moment, but not everything has to linger within it. This means that no unhappiness is a natural, or necessary, part of the perfectly present moment. For any sinking inner state to thrive, it must actually be carried into the now by someone who insists on clinging to his or her concept of happiness in the face of uncooperating life changes. And this is the key point in our lesson: *even though conflict may briefly appear in the present moment, it cannot dwell there anymore than it's the nature of a stream to carry the impression of a stone that sits in its flow.*

If there's friction in our lives, that conflict is the proof we're holding on to limiting beliefs which can never be a part of our freedom. Whatever psychological pains we may live with are the ones we just won't give up. And the only reason we won't release these loco-notions about ourselves is because we still wrongly believe that our ideas about who we are is who we are. They are not. They're only incomplete concepts, as is the troubled and temporary identity they provide. Let go of these concepts and we lose their pains.

This is the power of the perfectly present moment: *Dwelling within its incorruptible realm you awaken to the Truth of who you really are by repeatedly witnessing all that you are not.* There's no need to make this idea complicated, as the following clearly illustrates.

You are not that fear. You are not that worry. You are not that anger. You are not that doubt. You're never any of those clouds of thoughts or feelings that pass through and darken the sky of the perfectly present moment. And even as you bask in the light of this higher self understanding, and feel a new strength coming to you from beyond your mind, yet another realization awaits you.

Growing in awareness of the perfectly present moment is the same as awakening to your own True Nature: the Free Mind. *They are one and the same.* Your life and what is eternally *now* are one and the same *Truth*. And when you *know* that who you really are is new and fresh every moment, you also know that you never have to suffer over who you are—or are not— ever again. Know it!

Now it's up to you to transform these principles about the perfectly present moment into your own experience of their powers.

As an additional exercise, copy the next ten insights on a separate sheet of paper. Then, *using your own words*, rewrite each one in a new form pleasing to you. Using your mind in this way helps to take you from the world of these higher ideas into a higher world of new personal understanding, where you see at last that you need never suffer again.

1. Never hesitate to question those thoughts your own thinking tells you don't need to be questioned.

2. Freedom from the ties that bind follows outgrowing the need to always be in a struggle.

3. Who you really are is not, and cannot be, any thought you may have about yourself.

4. Dare to put aside for a moment what you want from life and, instead, dare to see what you're really getting.

5. Until you directly experience the *Truth* of something, you may think you know it—or that you have its powers—but all you really possess is one thought about another thought, and neither thought is the thing or its power.

6. The father of frustration, anger, and ultimate defeat is looking to the temporary for *a sense of permanence*.

7. The me mind loves to feel inadequate so it can imagine what it would be like to live without those painful feelings.

8. See that self comparison serves no purpose other than to produce self conflict, and then watch how this painful form of self interest fades away.

9. Call upon the power of the perfectly present moment to anchor you in a world where you can see that any suffering is a stone in the stream of your True Self.

10. Come awake as often as you can and consciously bring yourself back to the protective custody and permanence of the perfectly present moment.

CHAPTER 9

The Secret Of Making A New And True Beginning

O NE DAY AN ANNOUNCEMENT WAS POSTED. IT SAID there would be an open series of marathons and foot races comprised of various distances and degrees of difficulty. All who wished to test themselves against course, clock, and each other, were invited to compete for fabulous gifts and prizes, as well as for national recognition for being the best in their class.

Our hero couldn't wait to get to the races. He had trained long and hard, and he felt more than prepared. Whatever the challenges, he knew he would prevail.

At last the day came for the big event. There were thousands of well-conditioned men and women milling around, wearing outfits and jerseys every color of the rainbow. In the center of the staging area, ten or fifteen banners marked as many starting places. Between the mounting excitement and the confusion of all the runners dashing back and forth to find their particular staging areas, our hero felt as though he'd stepped into a washing machine that was doing colors on spin cycle.

The next thing he knew, a starting gun went off, catching him unprepared. And before he was even sure of how it happened, he was in the race of his life.

All his years of hard work were now on the line as he summoned himself to succeed as never before. And he rose to the occasion. One by one he ran past his competitors, as time itself seemed to disappear into the rhythm of his own clockwork breathing. But then, out of nowhere, the shouts from the cheering crowds lining the raceway began growing louder and louder. He knew he must be nearing the finish line. And with a final surge he crossed that invisible barrier that makes one person a winner—and all others just runners.

For some reason, the weight of the finish line ribbon stretching and breaking across his chest surprised him. It felt like a piece of velvet, and the strange weightless sensation captured his complete attention. But, seconds later, the sounds of all the yelling and cheering broke the spell and brought him back to the ache in his legs. But he had done it! He won!

He began jumping up and down, arms raised in the air, waiting for the crowds to surround him. But they were moving in another direction, away from where he was standing. The only person approaching him at the moment was an unsmiling volunteer official.

"Sir", the volunteer asked, "why are you jumping up and down?"

"I won the race," the man blurted out, behind gasps for air. He was somewhat stunned by the question.

"No, sir, you didn't," replied the official, obviously trying to be kind.

"What are you talking about?" the man fought to hold back his rising panic, "I crossed the finish line first!"

The official drew in a breath and spoke. He had seen this kind of anger before, and he knew he must break the news as gently as possible. "Sir, you have on a red jersey. This event was designated for runners wearing *blue*. I'm afraid you ran the wrong race."

What a shock! Our hero was unbelievably disappointed, but nevertheless undaunted. He returned to the starting gates to try again. And as he stood there, shaking out his arms and legs, he could feel fresh energy come to him as he envisioned himself winning the next race. A moment later another starting gun went off. And so did he.

Another hard-run race, and again, he was the very first to cross the finish line. But like a scene right out of a bad movie, another official came up to him bearing unwanted news. It seems that the race he'd just won was a qualifying heat only for persons of forty-five years and older. He looked down at his runners ID badge. It said he was only forty three. But right about then, he felt like the oldest man alive!

Over and over, the man in our story ran all-out races that day—spurred on by his visions of victory. Again and again, he crossed the finish line first—only to be told that he hadn't won that event either. Finally, one of the people in charge of the day's events walked up to him and said, "Having a pretty rough day today, aren't you?"

Too weary to even smile at this massive understatement, our hero just nodded and said, "But I don't really understand why this is happening to me."

All the official could do was look at him sympathetically. Then he spoke. "Sir, if you don't line up at the right starting place, how can you expect to win any race?"

The moral of this story holds a very valuable, but easily overlooked, inner life lesson. Its higher message applies to every department of our lives, but is especially meaningful when it comes to assuring us success in finding freedom from the ties that bind. As our next study will make abundantly clear: *without the right beginning, there can be no happy ending.*

The Secret Starting Place For All Happy Endings

Think about all the finish lines you've managed to cross in your lifetime where you thought you were an uncontested winner. Let's name a few:

1. "They said I was great!"

2. "She said she loved me!"

3. "I made the deal!"

4. "At last I own what I've always wanted!"

5. "The crisis is over at last."

6. "I beat the odds!"

7. "Now I know I'm a good and wise person."

Then comes that untimely, unkind, or unexpected event where you hear, in one way or another, from yourself or from someone else: "Sorry, you just ran the wrong race!"

Maybe you find out:

1. The one who you thought loved you really loves only the idea of being in love, which has to be renewed repeatedly with new loves.

2. That deal you made is slowly making you into someone you don't care for.

3. That crisis you thought you'd solved once and for all shows new signs of life.

In any one of these incredible instances, just like it happened to the runner in our story, victory is snatched from right out of your hands. All you're left holding is a sinking feeling.

Until now, all we've known to do in these key moments of defeat is to try and pull ourselves together, jump into another race, and hope things turn out better. But our study of the Free Mind shows we don't have to settle for just the hope of a happier finish. We can do better, much better. Certainty of succeeding in any of life's races is more than assured in the following understanding about the nature of making a true beginning.

There can be no starting place in our lives any truer than what our own awareness of the present moment permits.

This friendly fact tells us that our life direction, our actual destiny, *is determined by the level of our awareness* that attends the full range of each step we take. The next two examples prove this insight beyond the calling of any logic.

No one consciously takes a step in haste—*knowing* it will lead to waste. Neither would any man or woman consciously take a step in anger—if he or she *knew* the route just chosen would only lead to regrets.

These truths being self evident, we have to ask ourselves, "What's the force at the source of these false starting places? How is it our consciousness can be so compromised we're unable to see that a step taken in worry leads us not to the worry-free life, but only to the base of an active volcano called Mount Anxiety?"

It's crucial for us to understand the full meaning of the fact that the me mind—and the thrust of its habitual thinking—lives with its attention fixed, not on beginnings, *but on the end of things*. A quick self study in the form of a few honest questions proves this point.

Don't we always wonder what our lives will be like tomorrow? Aren't we forever dreaming about how different things will be once we win this or achieve that?

Don't we, in our mind's eye, perpetually walk towards a brighter moment to come, thinking about how good we'll feel once we're able to resolve some nagging situation?

We are betrayed every time when we set out on any journey—mentally, emotionally, or bodily—with our eyes fixed on *where we think we're going*, rather than *in the profitable awareness of where we are*. It's within this full awareness of where we are—which includes the alert observation of all our attending mental and emotional states—that is the *true beginning* we've been searching for all of our lives. Do you see why?

We don't ever have to worry about happy endings to any of our life stories if we're awake enough to refuse all unhappy beginnings. The Free Mind knows: *if we attend to the true beginning of whatever tasks or life travels lie ahead of us, their endings have to take care of themselves.*

THREE SECRET WAYS TO START YOUR LIFE OUT FRESH

Here are three new and true beginnings you can start with today that will put you in the right place for leaving old self defeating choices behind you for good.

1. Each time you find yourself face to face with some overbearing man or woman who in some way intimidates you, dare to make this new and true beginning: *act toward that person in exactly the way you want to act, and not in the way you think he or she expects you to.*

Within the guidelines of being kind and true, speak to that person as though you are completely free to say

156

what you feel, for you are. What any individual may think about what you have to say is not your concern. So let this false concern go.

This highly personal act of independence will likely cause you to tremble. That's alright. And should your shakiness become visible, proceed anyway. This true beginning will reveal that the cause of your unhappy endings with others has *never* been in what they've demanded of you, but rather within your own impossible and conflict-creating demands on yourself: that you be in charge of your own life *and*, at the same time, please everyone that asks you to do so.

2. The next time you begin to feel any conflict or confusion over some shaky situation that won't go away, dare to make this new and true beginning: *refuse to cave in to any painful inner prompting that urges you to just "get things settled."*

Deliberately defy those clamoring thoughts and feelings that want to send you on a search outside of yourself for peace of mind. This true beginning will help you to see that bringing an end to conflict must begin and end *within you*. Look nowhere else!

No snap or desperate decision made in conflict can ever resolve any shaky inner state, because part of any conflict is the fear of making a wrong choice, and fear is at the root of your shakiness, not the solution to it.

3. Any time someone criticizes or corrects you, dare to make this new and true beginning: *go against your habitual urge to defend yourself.*

Instead of reacting with heated resistance to something you don't want to hear about yourself, just *listen* to what's being said. This true beginning gives you the opportunity to see what you need to see about yourself. And here's a good guideline for evaluating moments such as these. The more you want to resist the things being said about you, the more you need to hear those very words. So don't criticize back, either out loud or under your breath. If you meet these moments with an argument, you've already lost.

Remember, there's always something to learn from something said that stings, even if its just to discover that you're still being tripped up by the long shadow of your own falsely inscrutable image.

THE VICTORY OF THE PRESENT MOMENT

Thinking, or hoping, that any destination we have in mind is going to be superior to where we're presently standing, is exactly why we're still standing in that same place where we have to hope that some tomorrow will be better.

Before we can change our destination and arrive in that higher world we want, before we can ever start out in that new direction that leads to liberation, we must *wake up* to the steps we're being given to take by a nature whose favorite direction is down. That's why I urge you to read the following portion of this chapter as though it holds the keys you need to change your destiny, for it does.

Victory over our own lower nature, the me mind, and ultimate contact with the Free Mind, is *now or never*. Patient exploration of this idea will prove itself invaluable to our inner studies.

Your True Nature is the same as the perfectly present moment. Using different words to arrive at the same meaning, we can also say that the *now* is our Celestial Nature: our Real Home. And because the *now* is forever new, your True Nature is always new too, which means that *who you really are* and the *now* are one and the same reality.

These revelations tell us that our innermost home exists in a state of constant creation, a secret world locked in a dynamic process of perpetual construction and destruction, living and dying and living again. All of which is happening *now*. The incredible implication of this inner discovery paves the way for the insights and the powers we need to effect true self transformation. Follow closely the next two key ideas.

The perfectly present moment is both the seed of *who you are and of your experience of now*.

And just as you can't separate *who you are* from your experience of *now*, neither can you separate *now from the real moment of change*. They are the same. There is a higher message hidden in this paragraph if you know where to find it, but the following sentences tell us its secret.

You can't end conflict later. You can't stop being sad, or cruel, or angry, or scared, or anxious later. And make this follow up point as clear as you can for yourself: *later does not exist in reality.*

Only to the me mind does the concept of later have any merit. This self created, false concept of time allows it to create yet another you in another time when, according to *its* prophecy, you'll be a wiser, stronger, and generally superior individual. But the Free Mind knows for you to experience the miracle of real inner transformation, to step up to a superior life level, you must no longer think in terms of *how you'll be next time*.

The Free Mind understands, as we must, that a change in nature is immediate; *it is now*. Or it won't be at all. And so it's imperative to meet each moment of your life with this realization: it's only what you do *right now* that is the seed of change. And in the endless beauty and mystery of what is the *now*, this same seed of change is also the seed of a New Self. Here's why this is true. *If you choose to change right now, then you won't have to worry about how to be different next time!*

In fact, choose to change *now*, and that moment will never come for you to worry about how to be better next time. Again, here's why. Your conscious choice for real change in the *present* moment automatically cancels the need for a better you in a better future. *All will be better for you now*, which is the only time it really matters!

USE THE POWER OF THE PRESENT MOMENT FOR SELF TRANSFORMATION

Make it your moment to moment practice to stay awake, and to watch for all the opportunities that your own *now* presents. Keep your efforts personal, practical, and to the point. If your inner work doesn't transform the whole of your life into a more relaxed, amazing, and uplifting experience, then you're dreaming, not changing.

To help you begin this important process of using the power of the present moment for personal transformation, the remainder of this chapter is designed to reveal the countless opportunities each day presents for you *to be free now*.

I've created a list of thirty ways in which your awareness of the power of *now* can transform each challenging life moment into a new and true beginning for you. Learning how to use these moments leads to real inner change, which is the same as being in command of your own destiny.

Here's extra encouragement. Your effort to understand these important studies helps turn their revelations into a part of your own evolving nature. And as you awaken to this Higher Life within yourself, you naturally attract higher, and happier events. There is no such thing as a wasted step when your final destination is self transformation.

Thirty Keys To Change Your Destiny

1. Now is always the time to: *Step out of the rush and into your own life.*

   Special Insight: Dare to slow down. Just do it. Here's help. See that, even at a million miles an hour, anxious thoughts and feelings *still take you nowhere.* To find what is timeless, dare to live as though you have all the time in the world. Step out of the rush. Step out *now.*

2. Now is always the time to: *Take responsibility for your life experience.*

   Special Insight: The way you feel toward what you meet in life is a direct expression of *who you are.* And *who you are* is exactly the same as what you secretly value. Seeing that *you feel the way you do because you treasure what you do* is what it means to take responsibility for your life.

3. Now is always the time to: *Refuse to be self compromising.*

   Special Insight: Drop any thought or action that creates conflict in the present moment for the promise of a better feeling to come. Your True Nature is *now. There is no later.* You can't be divided *and* be content. Choose to be whole. Begin by consciously refusing to compromise yourself.

4. Now is always the time to: *Remember you're not the only one in the world.*

Special Insight: It may feel like it, but you're not the only one who suffers! That's why you must not be afraid to take a good look at—and really consider—another human being. This will help you be less wrongly concerned with the way *you feel about yourself*—which will come as welcome relief. Remember, you're not the only one in the world.

5. Now is always the time to: *Go beyond the best that you think you can.*

Special Insight: Anybody can do what everybody else does—which is usually the minimum to get the maximum. Do more. Take the step you're sure you can't. You'll discover that the "you" who could not *is only a thought* that believes it cannot. See this. Then get going beyond yourself.

6. Now is always the time to: *Realize there's no gain in blame.*

Special Insight: When your feet ache because your shoes are too tight, you don't complain that someone else made you put them on. So why blame another when *it's your feelings that are hurting you?* If wearing painful emotions means *you* have to bear their pressure, then dare to drop them. You'll feel much better. There's no gain, only pain, in blame.

7. Now is always the time to: *Have a light spirit.*

   Special Insight: The heart tends to feel heavy when the mind says things aren't the way they ought to be. But *your True Nature* is neither thought nor emotion. You are *spirit.* And your spirit is always light-hearted. It knows better than to look for or find itself in a dark thought. Look at life through its eyes. Be light-spirited.

8. Now is always the time to: *Step down as judge.*

   Special Insight: The easiest thing in the world is to walk around unconsciously feeling superior to everyone you meet. But with what do you measure? A critical spirit? A judgmental mind? What kind of eyes have to look down on another to convince themselves of up? Step down as judge.

9. Now is always the time to: *Face those fearful feelings.*

   Special Insight: There is really no such thing as a shaky situation, so any time you start to tremble, don't look *around you* for the fault: *look inward.* It's the inner ground you're standing on that isn't solid. Any weakness faced by looking in this new direction becomes the foundation of a new strength. Face those fearful feelings. Fearlessness follows.

10. Now is always the time to: *Help someone else go higher.*

Special Insight: There's no such thing as a separate self, so anything you do to encourage another person to do better, or go farther, is the same as helping yourself go higher. Give yourself a lift up. Try a little kindness, even if you're not feeling that way at the moment. A kind feeling will follow. Help someone go higher.

11. Now is always the time to: *Release all resentments.*

    Special Insight: It's important for you to see that holding on to some hurt, or hatred, over what others may have done to you in the past, makes *you* their slave *in the here and now.* Is that what you want? Learn to ask for something new by refusing to relive what's been tearing at you. This higher request releases you from raging resentments.

12. Now is always the time to: *Do what is true regardless of the consequences.*

    Special Insight: Choosing what's true in spite of fearing what that choice may cost you is the same as giving yourself a fearless life. Nothing you're afraid of losing can ever be the source of your fearlessness. Do what's true regardless of the consequences. All you can lose is the fear.

13. Now is always the time to: *Let the empty space fill itself.*

    Special Insight: Nothing you've ever done has filled the emptiness you feel inside, *so stop giving yourself empty things to do. Leave the space empty.* This allows it to *fill itself*—which it wants to do—with something you can't give yourself—*the end of feeling empty*. Stay out of it. Don't fill the emptiness. Let the empty space fill itself.

14. Now is always the time to: *Stop explaining yourself to others*.

   Special Insight: The only difference between the need to endlessly explain your life to others and feeling as though you have to excuse yourself for being alive is that, while you're explaining yourself, at least it feels as though you have a good reason for being excused. You're not required to explain yourself to anyone. Stop *now*.

15. Now is always the time to: *Laugh in the face of defeat*.

   Special Insight: It's a fact that defeat is nothing but a bad memory. And no memory has any *real* life of its own. This means that the only time you have to feel the pain of any defeat *is if you ask for it*—by going into troubled thought about some painful *past* loss. You can have the last laugh on defeat. Stay in the present moment. Learn to laugh *now*.

16. Now is always the time to: *Follow what you love*.

   Special Insight: Put what you love *first*. The rest of your life will take care of itself because *love always finds a way*. Love never considers fear. And with love as your guide, your success in life is assured since its nature *is already* the perfect prize. Follow what you love. You're sure to find a happy heart.

17. Now is always the time to: *Start your life all over.*

    Special Insight: Any time you choose, you can start your whole life over. And you can have just as many new beginnings as you're willing to leave behind you *all of your ideas about yourself.* That's what it means to start all over. Life can only be as new as *you choose to be.* Wake up. Start your life over *now.*

18. Now is always the time to: *Keep your chin up.*

    Special Insight: Even if all of your thoughts are going that way, tell your chin not to fall down. As it obeys, it gives a message to your head, "Hold yourself up high!" And so your head helps your eyes to keep looking forward, where they can see, at last, that your thoughts are often blind. *Keep your chin up.* Consciousness likes heights. Dare to follow!

19. Now is always the time to: *Let it go.*

    Special Insight: You've been trying to run your own show and, so far, it's pretty much been just a nightmare with entertaining intermissions! Let something higher have its hand at directing your life. *Let your show go.* Then watch for a happy ending coming soon.

20. Now is always the time to: *Stop looking outside of yourself.*

    Special Insight: Your life is only as complete as you are. No more, no less. Looking to relationships, your work, or even happy events for a feeling of self wholeness is like trying to put a smile on your face in the mirror—*while you're still frowning*. Being complete is first an understanding, and *then* a feeling. Stop looking outside of yourself. Seek the understanding. Seek it *within*. The feeling will follow.

21.   Now is always the time to: *Have your own life.*

Special Insight: There is no pleasing the fear you may displease others. Allowing what *others may feel* about what you want—*to change the way you feel about that same want*—is like believing someone else can put on your sweater, and that you'll feel the warmth! The only real pleasure comes from *knowing* that you have your own life. Take your life back *now*.

22.   Now is always the time to: *Put your life in perfect order.*

Special Insight: Without the raindrop there is no ocean. The river runs to the sea because each stream finds, and fills, its course. *There is an order.* From the small is born the mighty, and the small is small no more. Remember each day of your life, there's *already* an order. Let go into its flow. And there you'll find you're small no more.

23.   Now is always the time to: *Jump into the battle.*

Special Insight: True strength is the flower of wisdom, but its seed is *action*. To learn, you must jump into the battle. Fear not. You can't be hurt in *this* fight. Any weakness voluntarily met *is the same as greeting a greater strength*. Never let a fearful thought keep you from this new strength. Enter the battle *now!*

24. Now is always the time to: *Discover the difference between your head and your heart.*

Special Insight: You can't think yourself into happiness, but you *can* sink yourself with a single dark thought. Right, bright emotions spring from the heart. Heavy feelings can't exist without the presence of negative thoughts. This means *sad states are just a trick of the mind.* To see through any state of sadness, see the difference between the head and the heart.

25. Now is always the time to: *Look up!*

Special Insight: A lamp without a light is as useless as a bottomless bucket. So too is this life empty without a sense of the sacred. The celestial is always present. Why wait until you feel down before you think to look up? You can always glimpse the higher, but you have to remind yourself to look in the right direction. Look up! Look *now.*

26. Now is always the time to: *Get one thing done.*

Special Insight: Never mind how much there is to do. Or how hard some task appears to be. *Get one thing done!* Then *take that step again.* Consciously brush aside any other concerns. Do what's in your power. *Refuse to deal with what's not.* The most beautiful tapestry in the world begins and ends with one of ten thousand *individual* threads.

27. Now is always the time to: *Go quiet.*

Special Insight: The frantic search for any answer only delivers answers on the same frantic level. Don't be afraid to go quiet. *It's OK to not know.* Knowing that you don't know what to do puts you where you need to be *to learn.* Just as you can see farther on a clear day, new understanding flowers in a quiet mind. Go quiet *now.*

28. Now is always the time to: *Separate the fact from the fear.*

    Special Insight: The fact of any problem, and the fearful feeling about it, are totally separate issues *appearing as one.* They merge only in a thought telling you one can't exist without the other, which is like thinking you can't feel a chill without having the plague. The fear you feel over any situation *is the same as your demands upon it.* Separate the fact from the fear *now.*

29. Now is always the time to: *Catch yourself in the act.*

    Special Insight: The problem with acting out any role is that *your life can't be both a show and be real.* Wanting and winning the attention of others with a performance of any kind doesn't make the performer real, any more than smiling at yourself in the mirror makes you loving. Life is only real *when you are.* Catch yourself in the act. Then just drop it.

30. Now is always the time to: *Know that the time is always now.*

    Special Insight: You can't change the kind of person you are later. *There is no later.* It's always now or never. You can't be kind *later.*

And you can't learn *later*. But even if there seem to be times when you can't succeed with starting your life over, keep this one Truth in mind. You can always start over *again*. The time to change your destiny is *now*!

A SPECIAL NOTE TO THE READER

For those readers who are interested in making the important extra effort that turns these teachings into the inner triumph of a higher destiny, the following course of study and action is advised.

Work closely with each of these moment-of-change studies. Give your complete attention *to one* lesson at a time, for at least a full day. Make it your intention to apply that inner lesson at every available opportunity. You'll discover that these teachings offer a source of healing support in any crisis or circumstance, and in every relationship.

Make it your aim to stay awake in as many challenging moments as you can—where it's possible for you to change your destiny—*by choosing to change the direction of your inner life in the now.*

One last note: succeed just once—*with any one* of these unique exercises—*and you'll never be the same again.* All will be *new* for you. Both for the fact of your victory over the time nature of the me mind—and for your new knowing that now tells you: yes, you *can* change your destiny.

CHAPTER 10

Winning The Final Freedom

SELDOM DO WE KNOW A GREATER NEED FOR MAKING A fresh start than in those mind-numbing moments when we find ourselves feeling thrown for a loss. But, for reasons still to be revealed, this unsought after sensation—what feels like life having stripped away something cherished from our grasp—doesn't always come upon us in a recognizable way. Many times, maybe most, there's no resounding bang at all before the fall.

The feeling of loss can be very quiet. So subtle, in fact, is its nature at times, that we often suffer this feeling of ourselves going empty without even becoming conscious of why we're hurting in the way that we are. Let's identify a few of these unsuspected moments where we haven't a clue there's been a thief about who has left us with less.

We Feel The Pain Of Loss:

1. Each time the smallest thought passes through our minds about what we could have had, been, or done differently in our lives.

2. Each time we argue with someone.

3. When others fail to see the intelligence or beauty in our thinking.

4. Whenever we detect the smallest negative change in someone's attitude towards us.

5. If someone even hints that his or her formerly pleasing picture of us is not as bright as it used to be.

All that's left of these otherwise undetected events—which put us at a loss without even knowing why we feel that way—is an unconscious, invisible residue of fear; a faint psychic trembling which tends to taint every area of our lives with distasteful timidity, born of the neurotic suspicion that in some way, life is conspiring to take something away from us.

But real Life is not about to try and diminish itself. And we are of that Being. Life is about development, enrichment, and fulfillment that begins with our Spirit. If there's grief, if there's the pain of a loss, that moment has to be a part of life, *and a part of its growth*. Looking upon the loss of anything as though it means *the end* of it, is the same as believing falling autumn leaves mark the end of the trees.

Clearly, we must learn to see our own lives in a whole new light. We need a higher understanding of how to look at the pain of loss, one that won't leave us its captive, but that will show us the secret of cooperating with life, and how to transform our seeming losses into the higher lessons they're intended to be.

The good fortune is that such an elevated under-standing already exists. Read on and discover the secret of how you can take the shaking aching out of any loss, and transform it into the seed of self libera-tion. Gather all the facts about to be presented. Follow them all the way to freedom.

Why You Don't Have To Own Those Feelings Of Loss

The Free Mind is never thrown for a loss. But just because this higher nature doesn't go into a tailspin each time some part of our life drops the other shoe doesn't mean that the nature of the Free Mind is uncar-ing or disconnected from the goodness of our own. To the contrary, the real joys of life are the natural, effort-less expressions of our own True Nature. But these pure joys don't belong to us as our possessions, any-more than a bird *owns* the freedom of the open skies through which it soars.

Even so, many of the men and women I speak to have more or less reconciled themselves to accept the negative notion that just to be alive means they're going to ache over some kind of loss. And in my meet-ings with groups of seekers about the possibility of learning to live without the pain of loss, most everyone is *both attracted and frightened* by the idea of it.

In our ongoing discussions, such as the one that fol-lows, these divided feelings always provide abundant energy for a stimulating, inwardly healing dialogue.

"I must admit, the thought of going through life without aching over a loss of some kind is a very wel-come notion. But the whole idea of *not* feeling loss also frightens me in a way that's hard to describe. I mean, what kind of person would I be if I *didn't* feel bad when I lose something—or someone—near and dear to me?"

This is a very important question, and its patient investigation will give us a whole new way to look at the nature of loss. But the sensitive issues raised by such an investigation require we suspend those strong feelings of ours which attend the subject of loss and sorrow. Are you willing?

"If there's really a way to take the torment out of personal loss, I want to know about it. The most difficult moments of my life have always come on the heels of learning I've just lost something important to me, or that such a loss is imminent. So yes, I want to learn. Where do we begin?"

With a question. If you see a person who you don't know, and he's looking around frantically for something he's lost, is his loss of any real, or personal, concern to you?

"Generally speaking, I suppose not. But what's the point?"

The first of our lessons concerns the idea of *possession*. The man's loss in our illustration is of no concern to *you* because whatever it is he's lost doesn't *belong to you*.

"Alright, that's obvious. But, please continue."

Before we can begin to understand, and then dismiss, the feelings of pain and emptiness which always seem to shadow our losses, we must become aware of those invisible inner mechanisms that create our sense of attachment, of ownership. In other words, we can't look into the nature of loss without investigating *the idea of gain*. Loss and gain are really two sides of the same coin, just as are win and lose, love and hate. *They are opposites*. Can you see you can't have one of these concepts without the other? What power would that self punishing idea of failure have without its rewarding opposite which we call success?

"Sure, that's clear. But it sounds as though you're telling me that if I win something—or gain some advantages in my life—that at some predetermined point, I've got to lose these victories because defeat comes attached to them. Is that it? Sounds negative to me!"

No, that's not it at all. Believing it's written somewhere that you must suffer just because you find some joy in excellence, or in others, is like thinking that you can't enjoy the warmth of the sun without getting burned. It's just not true. And yet, our personal experience shows that our overall feelings of personal loss *at least* match those of our having gained something for ourselves, and perhaps more, especially if we're brave enough to take into account those invisible losses described at the outset of this chapter.

"Yes, I think I have to agree with you. This whole question of loss, and how little we understand it, runs deeper than we know. For instance, I suspect that beyond the actual heartache of those losses I've already learned to live with, I also live with the fear of losing what I haven't already lost. Can you imagine that?

"And I strongly suspect this kind of invisible fear is worse than anything I might actually lose, because its presence makes me wary of almost everything that seems to be bright and promising. I guess I just don't want to be hurt *again*, and this fear of loss tends to hold me back from openly committing myself to new opportunities and challenging relationships. Either I don't give them my best or I just refuse to enter those situations altogether. And I know that's not right.

"Is there really a way for me to transform these losses in my life into something self empowering, instead of just learning to live with what is inherently self punishing?"

Definitely! Let's take one well-studied step at a time. We're right on the verge of a very important discovery.

Imagine for a moment that you owned a pair of magic glasses which you were free to wear any time you thought you had lost something. Now, further imagine that through these glasses you could see, clearly, each time, that whatever it was you'd thought you'd lost, wasn't, *in fact*, really yours at all. What do you think would happen to the pain of your loss with such a new kind of sight?

"Well, I suppose I'd feel the same way I thought I would in the story of the man who had lost something that *wasn't mine*. In short, *I* wouldn't suffer over it. But that story was just an illustration. My life is real, as have been each of my losses. And yet, if there really was some new way to see my losses through magical lenses like those you've just described, everything about my life would be so different, so open and new."

Wouldn't that kind of life be something worth working for?

"By all means. Please tell me where to begin."

SEEING THIS IS FREEING YOURSELF FROM THE FOUNDATION OF FEAR

We have to start by asking ourselves very honestly: What is it we really want? What are we trying to accomplish with all our ambitions, our goals, our acquisitions of relationships, power, and possessions? What are we hoping to find at the end of each of these drives?

"Well, I can't answer for anyone else, but it seems obvious to me; I want to succeed. I seek the same silver-lining everyone else does: a happy and contented life. Aren't these natural wishes?"

Of course they are. But let me ask you a telling question. Has there ever been a time in your life when, for all of the gains you'd made, some unwanted event came along and made all that you had won for yourself seem meaningless? When, in spite of all that remained for you to be thankful for, your loss made you feel bitter or defeated?

"Sure, I've had times like that. But who hasn't? Besides, I don't give up easily. I just bounce right back."

If you owned an umbrella that every now and then turned into a watering can *while you were using it*, would you use it to keep you dry and out of the rain?

"Of course not, but I really don't see the connection."

What do you think these stressful times following your feelings of loss are trying to tell you?

"To tell you the truth, I never thought of them as carrying a message. But, based on what I do after I pick myself up and start over, I suppose their message to me is that I need to work harder."

But haven't you been doing just that all along? What exactly is it you hope to win for your repeated struggles?

"I see what you're getting at. What I want is to be in the position one day where nothing can take away—or threaten—what I've gained."

Then what you're calling your search for success is actually a search for security?

"No, that doesn't completely cover it for me. What about wanting the happiness and contentment we mentioned earlier?"

When is the joy of well-being more deeply experienced than in our moments of feeling most secure? And conversely the same holds true. When do things seem darkest if not in times of greatest doubt? What loss seems greater than the one which leaves us feeling most vulnerable?"

"I have no argument with this point. But what does it matter whether I call it searching for happiness, success, or as you put it, security? Isn't it all the same? What's the difference in a name?"

You're right. The problem doesn't lie within *what* we name as our security. As far as that goes, any name is as good as another. Our real dilemma is that all of these goals *and* their names *are given to us* by the me mind. And this level of our own mentality can *only think in the opposites*.

"I'm not sure I follow you. What do you mean that my mind can only think in the opposites?"

We touched on this important idea of the opposites earlier, when we mentioned how we measure our sense of success relative to our notions of failure. But now we need to look a little deeper. We need to understand what it is that creates these opposites in the first place. So, let's begin with the following insight: *thought, itself,* by its very nature, casts the thinker apart from what he or she is thinking about.

"Would you mind making this last idea a little clearer for me?"

This important insight about the nature of thought doesn't have to be confusing. A simple exercise you can do right now will tell the whole story. Then you'll see for yourself how thought divides.

Put this book down and let your eyes fall on something, anything, nearby. Now, try to notice what happens the instant your mind names the object or person you've sighted. *See* how your own thoughts *about it* actually *give you* an immediate *feeling of being separate from it*.

This discovery has immense implications. As long as our view of life is derived from this divisive thought nature, we can't help but see ourselves as being separate from the whole world around us. To *think* about a "you," there has to be a "me." This unconscious, but mistaken perception of our being separate from the whole of life, and everyone else in it, *is the foundation of fear*.

When we look out from eyes that see life in this divided fashion, we see ourselves as being alone. Not because we want to, but because the very way in which the me mind operates sets us adrift in a world where people, events, even inanimate objects, can only fall into only one of two categories: *everything is seen as being either for us, or against us.*

It's because of this strained "do or die" perception—wherein we forever see ourselves as being apart from life—that we're driven to seek security *in order to protect ourselves from it.*

"What you're saying is undoubtedly true, although I never saw my situation in this kind of light before. So what I've always called seeking security is really a form of looking for self protection. And yet, don't we need security? Don't we have to protect ourselves and our loved ones?"

Yes and no. Try to see the difference between *providing for* and *protecting* yourself. And while in today's quickly sickening society, these two activities seem to be increasingly related, I assure you that, spiritually speaking, the two have nothing in common. The former is a physical need which can be filled with simple things, while trying to protect yourself is a psychological state which knows no end. Now, add to this valuable insight the understanding that *you can't protect a fear* and you're very near discovering the secret of how to transform the pain of any loss into an act of self liberation.

"Everything in me senses we're headed in the right direction with this study, but I can't seem to see beyond my own feet! Please show me some more?"

Freedom From The Heartache Of Losing Any Love

If we look very closely at a moment of loss, regardless of its nature, you'll see that the underpinnings of your experience of this event are feelings of great *vulnerability*. We tend to feel at *risk* in a loss of any kind, even though when we *think* about that loss our mind will tell us that these concerns are not solely selfish.

"But aren't painful feelings natural when suddenly there's this hole left in your life?"

You may have lost something, even a loving relationship that was special to you. But the pain of your loss is not in the fact that person, position, or possession is gone from your life.

"What in the world do you mean? What else could make me feel that bad?"

Before we answer your question I want to remind you of something we agreed upon earlier. *It's impossible to lose something you never owned.* We don't own—no one owns—what we call our relationships, our appearance, our authority, intelligence, even our very own life.

"Of course you're right. This is starting to make sense. But why is there so much misery in a loss if we never owned what we thought we did? Just what is it we lose that makes us feel so badly?"

What we actually lose is an *image*, a carefully constructed mental picture of ourselves long-secured in place by someone or something that helps us to see ourselves—or feel about ourselves—the way we imagine ourselves to be. And with that person, position, or possession no longer in place to sustain that image, our pain is in the loss of that imaginary self.

"You say all that's been lost is an image, but how can that be? Something that was once there isn't anymore, whatever that something may have been. It's gone! How can you say there was no loss?"

Because there was none. Permit me to explain. There may have been a *change* in your life, but *this change is not the pain of loss.*

We can't own something that's in constant change, and all of life is exactly that: ceaseless, eternal change. But the me mind is compelled to seek what it calls security. So it creates mental images it can hold in place. *Images that don't change.*

Again, *real life is change.* At some point, real events won't allow these false images to remain intact. Then we can no longer deny reality its course. Something has to give. Mental pictures—no matter how well conceived—are always the first to break up in any shakeup. It's the collapse of these images that we call loss.

"I can see how what you've said must be true, like the feeling that comes over you when discovering someone you thought you could bank on is actually a thief of sorts, or finding out at the most crucial moment that you're not as strong as you always pictured yourself as being. These shocks always hurt!

"I can also understand, to some degree, how any time an image crumbles, it's going to feel just terrible. But what about the loss of a loved one? He or she is just gone, out of your life forever. What about that pain? Are you saying this deep heartache isn't real as well? That losing someone you love is just losing an image?"

No, of course not. There is pain. And this pain is most certainly real. But again, we must remind ourselves—even in the face of this awful emptiness—that *all* of our painful feelings of loss belong to a lower level of mind, the me mind, whose thought nature it is to create a world around it *from which it is ever apart.*

But, *who you really are* can't lose anything because your True Nature, the Free Mind, is *one* with the whole timeless goodness of life. And it's impossible to lose yourself! When you know you can't really lose anything or anyone, if you understand there is no real division between you and the one you love or, for that matter, between you and love itself, then the heartache of loss simply ceases to exist for you.

TURN ANY SORROW INTO A HIGHER SELF HEALING

"I really do understand how these ideas are true, and that they're beautiful. But I don't live at this higher level of awareness. And yet, I want to! More than anything! But I don't know how. Where do I begin?"

Right where you are.

"What do you mean? Where is *that*?"

At the level of feeling each loss as though you've just lost a part of yourself.

"Wait a minute! I don't understand. That's the very life level I want to lose!"

Which is why you must start there. From this moment forward, each time you feel a loss of some kind, meet it in this bold new way. Your higher actions will transform that loss into the seed of self liberation.

After each setback, *regardless* of its nature, leave that aching, empty space within you empty and aching. Your new aim is *not to fill it* with one recognizable thing: no plans, no anger, no fears, no regrets, hopes or dreams. Let no mental or emotional pictures of any kind rush in to bridge that gaping hole in your heart.

This inner action doesn't mean you try and push any of these pains away.

Denial is just another way in which we secretly try to fill the aching space. Instead, remain quietly aware of the pain *and* of that part of you that would make the ache go away by creating some new image to cling to in the storm. Have *nothing* to do with either these mental creations, nor with their creator. Both originate from the low level of the me mind that's the source of your sadness. If *you* allow this divided nature to fill the space, you'll only have to fill it again and again.

"I'm not sure how to put this, but if I don't answer the emptiness, if I don't do something to soothe my pain, then *what will*? You can't be telling me that we have to learn to live with heartaches?"

Don't you see? *You're already living that way!* Now it's time for you to die to this pained level of mental life so that you may consciously realize another higher level of your own being: the Free Mind. You can live from a new self that doesn't have to go searching for security because its lofty nature is *already whole*. Each conscious refusal, to answer the ache of any loss with your own security-restoring solutions, invites reality to flood in and fill that space. And reality *is never thrown for a loss*.

This very special approach to meeting each loss, and its grief, helps place you above your own habitual painful responses. Which is a lot better then carrying them around. The reason you can take this brave new inner action is because now you know: your sense of loss—that terrible empty experience—is only present within you because *you've forgotten who you really are*.

But all fearful feelings fade in the light of true self understanding. And as you grow in the awareness of your own timeless nature, a new strength makes itself known to you, within you. Calm and confidence come into your heart. Insight increases. You see your life has never been about winning and losing. Now you understand. Everything, everyone, each event, is cause for the exploration, discovery, and celebration of your essential self.

And this realization both teaches and cheers you. For your new knowing reveals that each of your seeming losses is really a secret invitation, *a call for you to go higher and higher, a summons from the Free Mind to enter into its fully liberated life and live forever without the fear of loss.*

TEN TRUTHS THAT PROVE YOU HAVE NOTHING TO LOSE

See if you can discover what these ten truths share in common. Use this important section to show you how to transform yourself from being someone who may be afraid of loss into someone who sees there's really nothing to lose ... and the whole of life to gain.

1. Counting on the way you *think* to rescue you from the way you *feel* is like running to the unsubmerged part of a sinking ship, and clinging to it for safety.

2. Start seeing that no mental or emotional suffering belongs to you, and that its presence in your life is invasive—*not* essential.

3. Learn to challenge your own thinking on the basis of what *you know about it*—and not from what *it's always trying to tell you about you.*

4. The present moment, free from thought and desire, is the only real treasure worth seeking because it alone contains all there is that has no opposite.

5. Reflect often during your day what it would be like to live from the *allness* of the Free Mind, instead of from the smallness of the me mind.

6. Believing that getting what you want will somehow bring an end to your wants is like thinking that a rock rolling down a hill is going to stop somewhere along the way to enjoy the view.

7. The next time you start to feel sad, or bad, about some loss, come wide awake and be shocked that only a moment before you were sure that you needed to suffer.

8. The difference between unnatural wants and natural needs is that the former drives you through your life, while the latter nurtures it.

9. See that every thought-projected pleasure contains its own hidden, painful opposite, and you'll soon know the incorruptible higher pleasure of not being a pain to yourself.

10. Waking up to the silent strength and fearless life of the Free Mind is the same as waking up to all you're intended to be.

CHAPTER 11

Crossing The Threshold Into
The Free Mind

WE'VE LEARNED AS MUCH AS WORDS AND KNOWLEDGE alone can give us about the true nature of the ties that bind, and the secrets of self liberation. Our studies have delivered us to the threshold of a unique inner event, a challenging moment in each person's spiritual journey along the way to the liberated life.

Before we can go any higher, before we can realize the self release we seek, we must take *that next real step* in our own spiritual development. And yet, even as our awareness grows that we must take this new step beyond ourselves, we also realize the immense difficulty of it, for we remain unable to see past the me mind and the haunts of its old wants—wants which we now know, even if realized, still can't take us anywhere higher, or farther, than to just another low-level want!

Over eight hundred years ago, the illuminated Sufi poet Hakim Sanai wrote about the challenges of being in this same difficult spiritual position. In *The Walled Garden of Truth*, the seeker is told: "As long as you cling to your self, you will wander right and left, day and night, for thousands of years; and when, after all that effort, you finally open your eyes, you will see your self, through inherent defects, wandering round itself like the ox in a mill; but, if, once freed of your self, you finally get down to work, this door will open to you within two minutes."

How do we cross over into a freedom which we know we cannot—*and must not—name for ourselves with our present level of mind?* How do we go further than we are when we don't really understand what it means to take ourselves there?

If you *know* you can't take yourself any farther but, at the same time, *you know there is still farther to go,* then you must permit yourself to be taken there by something that is *not you as you presently know yourself.*

Reaching this unthinkable yet conclusive level of understanding is to stand at the threshold of the Free Mind. But having made it to this elevated entrance that opens into our own Higher Nature, we now must find our way beyond it. *Knowing the truth about freedom and being free in truth are as different as are a bottle of sea water and the ocean from which it was taken.*

STAND IN THE "UNTHINKABLE PLACE" THAT HAS BEEN PREPARED JUST FOR YOU

One of the most consistent stumbling blocks standing in the way of self awakening lies within an unconscious conviction that a well-tended collection of insights about the awakened life is the same as being an inwardly liberated man or woman. But, having evidence of the existence of the Free Mind, regardless of how conclusive, *is not* the same as *living from the intel-*

ligence of it. The words of noted spiritual author Dr. Paul Brunton help complete our finding and give us important instruction as well. "Words only hint at this Reality, but they do not, cannot explain it. Truth is a state of being, not a set of words. The cleverest argument is no substitute for personal experience. We must experiment if we are to experience."

If you persist along these essential lines of self study which lead to lasting self liberation, you'll realize, more times than you wish that, in spite of all you've come to know about your own True Nature, all you really possess of this great essence is a lot of *ideas* about it.

There's no mistaking these moments. Never is it so painfully obvious that even your most ennobling spiritual idea is only just that—an idea—than in some moment of need, when you look to that idea to lift you above an inner storm, and all it does is turn into part of the downpour! Each time this happens you'll feel abandoned, *but don't discourage*. Abandon instead any and all discouraging feelings. Your unwanted but nevertheless great discoveries about what's real and genuine, about what can be counted on, and what's to be dismissed are vital to your continuing inner development.

As difficult as it may be to grasp, especially when amplified by the humiliation of seeing just how blind you've been to your own unsuspected ignorance, these moments when your defeat looms largest are the ones you've been preparing for all along. Yes! That's right. Here's why.

Before you can cross over into the realm of the Free Mind, your arrival at this new inner threshold demands you must leave your well-known world of ideas, of thought, and its level of self, the me mind, behind you. It is unthinkable. But equally clear: *you must let go of you*, even as it becomes clear that all you've ever been tied to, *and still are, is you.*

189

Have no fear of finding yourself feeling lost or spiritually stranded in this strange inner territory, a psychological world offering no known forward direction, and from where you know you can't go back. *All the spiritual courage and inner resolution you need to remain there, and triumph, is already right within you.* Look for it in your awakening understanding that there really is no other place for you to go. Persist in this place, and you'll discover its hidden promise.

Everything you need to be victorious in this spirit-based trial will be given to you. You're now standing at that one inner station where the Free Mind can, and will, make itself known to you. While it may not seem like it at the time, this place has been prepared just for you.

TO KNOW REAL FREEDOM YOU MUST GO BEYOND THE KNOWN

Our eyes and ears, thoughts and feelings, empower us to move freely through the extraordinary web of life of which we're a part. But these gifts of perception, as considerable as they may be, are more like a looking glass than they are the keys to that secret kingdom of freedom we seek. With their aid, we can *almost* see into, and so confirm, that innermost realm where our heart senses we belong. Yet these same significant senses have no power to help us cross over into our own timeless and free True Nature.

Nothing is more difficult than "knowing" that a grand newness awaits us, even as we find ourselves still firmly in the grip of old doubts and fears. What we do with these encounters of the truthful kind determines our success. How we proceed when denied our spiritual heart's desire is everything. A special story tells all.

Imagine a man who hears of a certain healing flower growing on a distant mountain. In spite of his many friends who tell him no such miracle occurs in nature, and that he's just fine the way he is, he knows in his heart something isn't right within him. And though not sure why, he's equally sure he needs this flower. So, in spite of everything, he begins his search.

When he at last reaches the foot of the mountain whose heights are rumored to bear the rare flower, he's surprised to find lots of people already gathered there, many of them claiming to sell the very blossom he wants.

But closer investigation proves it's not the actual flowers they're peddling, but only books about their healing petals. Everywhere he turns there are still others selling even more goods. There are detailed maps of the mountain, with the best paths to take, amulets to insure safe travel, and even an etiquette guide for bartering with those people living in the local hills, thought to know the secret way to the flowers hidden home.

But in all of these promises he finds only foolishness; no flower. So the next day he starts his climb. By himself.

Weeks later, after scaling dozens of rocky crests, through barren, waterless regions with freezing temperatures, he came to a bright, sun-warmed valley dotted with clear, sparkling artisan springs. His spirits soared for what his eyes beheld. But a moment later, they plummeted back to earth.

Poppies, wild roses, and countless other colorful blossoms were everywhere. It seemed to him that every flower imaginable must have been growing right there. Every flower, that is, except for the one that could heal. He wondered how this was possible. The sun warms every nook and cranny. Water is abundant. The soil's dark and rich. And yet, for all the evidence, nowhere does he see his heart's expectation. Still, this must be the place. Reason tells him so, as does his own heart.

And so he searches high and low, late into the day. And even as the sun descends, he persists, but with no luck. All he finds are his own thoughts telling him that he's foolish.

At last, as darkness falls, along with his defeated spirits, he turns to head back down the mountain. And even as he chooses his footfalls, his mind searches for ways to explain his failure to himself, and to the others he knows will ask him for his findings. Surely he can't tell them his search was in vain! If he's found nothing, what would that make him in their eyes? No, that would never do. But what else?

So, a story begins to take shape in his mind. After all, how many others have seen the part of the mountain he'd just visited? Who else but he knows anything at all about the hidden valley or, for that matter, what actually grows there? But right in the middle of his own dream to reconstruct his dignity, he remembers: these feelings aren't what he had come to the mountain to find. *He came to find the flower that heals.*

But what to do? His head and heart pull at him from two different directions. How could there be so much evidence, and yet no trace of the healing flower? But it's clear. He knows what he must do. He must return to the high mountain valley.

But this time, on his way back, he has to climb over his own mountainous doubts as well as jagged boulders. Still, one thing spurs him on, moving his feet one step at a time over the bruising, stony ground. Somewhere in that hidden valley is where he'll find the flower he needs. Of that much he's certain, *even if he doesn't know where or how.*

For the next full month he scours the valley floor. But he finds nothing. The occasional mountain storms that thunder over his head are nothing compared to the tempests raging in his own mind.

Finally, unable to look—or care—any more, he half sits, half falls down, in the middle of a small clearing. And it's right there that he passes the rest of that day and the next. Besides, he's so tired. And now there's nowhere else to go. But on the third day something unexpected starts happening. At first he isn't sure of his own eyes. Could it be? But of course!

Throughout the entire valley and all around him, delicate flowers begin breaking the surface of the soil, raising their tiny petals to the sun. A moment later, a long-forgotten fragrance stirs his heart. It's *the flower*. He reaches over and picks one: his *own*.

The next morning he awakens fully refreshed only to discover that all of the little flowers are gone, vanished. But he's not worried about their disappearance. He understands so much more now than he did just the day before. Now he knows these healing blossoms only bloom for a few moments on a schedule all their own. Then he looks down into his own carefully cupped hand. His flower remains. He breathes of it deeply. All is well.

The mental and emotional images written into this illustrative story are intended to take you beyond the words used to convey them. Review carefully the crucial four point summary and special inner life exercise that follows. Allow their higher lessons to lead you all the way to that rarest flower of all: spiritual self liberation.

1. Learn to go beyond even your own fear that there may not be a "beyond" to enter.

2. Meet the moment of having no future in sight, and refuse to close your eyes to create one.

3. You must learn to always keep your inner work headed higher, without relying on those parts of yourself that are always telling you what that direction may be. When thoughts

and feelings can no longer see, they would just as soon have you believe there's nothing beyond the limits of their vision.

4. Proceed, *in spite of your senses*, to call upon that new world within, the Free Mind. Go boldly beyond conviction, beyond confusion, beyond knowing.

THIS KEY UNLOCKS THE DOOR TO THE FREE MIND

Make this last exercise your constant companion. Within it I have summarized the most important lessons of this book.

The next time you run into some familiar blockage or begin to feel unsuited to face some new and difficult personal challenge, don't do what you've always done before. *Don't try to think your way around it*. You no longer want a way around your troubles because what goes around, comes around! What you want is to grow beyond the level of that disturbance. And to do that, *you must not act from it*.

So don't allow yourself to be pulled down into any anxious concern or confusion over not knowing what to do about your present condition. What you really want is an insight into your situation, not a fight with it. The two have nothing in common. So make it clear to yourself once and for all: *nothing that hounds you can help you*.

Draw yourself back from your usual thinking. Quietly observe the me mind race around looking for the shelter of a conclusion it can recognize. Have nothing to do with its frantic motion.

You've gone as far as you can go with what you know. Now it's time to *know* that, so that you can let *what you know go*, and let something unthinkable occur to you. Just relax.

Pressuring yourself to come up with a happy ending to a sad or shaky situation only goes to show you still believe that you can resolve these troubles. But if you could have, you would have by now. Besides, the me mind wants you to confuse these feelings of pressure for being some kind of proof of personal progress. It's done its job well. After all these years you're afraid to live without this feeling of habitually prodding yourself, for fear that without it, you might get stuck! The solution here is to see that, in fact, *you are stuck! This powerful insight releases you from the pressure of wanting anything from yourself.*

Now you've done *what you can do*. You've prepared the stage, your own mind, for the arrival of the Free Mind. And this royal nature will arrive. But learn to expect it in the unexpected. To paraphrase the New Testament: be ever watchful for you don't know when—or how—something higher will make itself known to you.

There may come a flash of insight, a clear glimpse into some self created cause of your own continuing inner captivity. Or, perhaps, a sudden and sweet deep sense of wholeness will sweep through you, a quiet but profound intuition, wherein you know yourself, for that moment, *to be one* with all of that life pulsating around and within you.

However that Light breaks into the darkened room of self, consider each brief illumination as an appointed messenger, a heavenly herald sent in advance of a greater freedom to come. Learn to embrace each appearance, for regardless of what may be revealed— to you or about you—these insights are not unlike the sound of the shouts of liberation heard always just before the arrival of the liberating forces. A new freedom always follows. Now, follow it.

SIXTY INSIGHTS TO STRENGTHEN YOU ALONG THE WAY TO SELF LIBERATION

You are never required by real life to accept any inner condition that compromises your spiritual wish to be free. To strengthen your wish, carefully consider each of these sixty summarizing insights. The clearer you can make your wish to find freedom from the ties that bind, the sooner it will be granted.

1. Your decision to be free begins right *now*.

2. Never believe that you must learn to live with anything that torments you.

3. Self compromise is the same as self sorrow.

4. All the pure powers that form the foundation of true freedom are already in place *within you*.

5. Any wish to appear strong in the eyes of others is a secret weakness.

6. Canceling the confusion of painful self contradiction *begins* with becoming conscious of it within yourself.

7. There's no such thing as a right reason for a wrong feeling.

8. The Free Mind dwells in a world where there is no such thing as defeat.

9. Stop thinking in terms of *where you want to go*, and begin thinking in terms of *who you need to be*.

10. Believing that anxious thoughts and feelings can restore order to your life is like using a chain saw to fold your laundry.

11. Drop all thoughts that anxiously instruct you to give yourself away today, so that tomorrow you might have what you need to own yourself.

12. A change of nature *is not* evolutionary, it is voluntary.

You Are Much More Than You Think You Are

13. Believing that who you are is any one of the millions of thoughts and feelings that pass through you is like thinking that a shooting star has the same nature as the open heavens which it flashes through and across.

14. First recognize, and then release yourself, from any feeling of responsibility for some other person's angry state.

15. Thinking you can resolve a crisis by rearranging the conditions surrounding it at the moment of eruption is like trying to landscape an active volcano in the hope that resurfacing its slopes will defuse its underground pressure.

16. One of the Free Mind's unfailing strengths is it has no fear for which way the world turns.

17. The cleverness of the me mind is not the same as consciousness.

18. Nothing is more rewarding than discovering your own nature is the reward you've been seeking.

19. Your awareness of any inner disturbance must precede your freedom from it; this is the one, true order upon which self liberation is founded.

20. Learning to love the Light is the same as self illumination.

21. The only thing that disappears when we close our eyes to something that's holding us down is our chance to be free of it.

22. Don't try to become great; be great *now*, and discover that excellence is a reward you don't need others to confirm.

23. Man's true condition is that he needs to be rescued, but dreams he is the rescuer.

24. Wasting your time in anxious worry over what you may not have is a good way to waste what you need to get it.

Change The Way You See Your Life

25. Learn to use life's shocks to see that you never collide with anything but yourself.

26. The Free Mind wants you to know that the only thing that disturbs you is the way *you've been taught to think about yourself*.

27. The Free Mind contains the me mind, and is able to direct it; the me mind doesn't even possess itself, but only thinks it does.

28. The me mind isn't even for *itself*, so how can it possibly be for you?

29. Going into painful, personal conflict doesn't prove you want a solution to your problem, it only prevents you from seeing that your first solution has always been to go into conflict.

30. Seeking the Free Mind is not an abandonment of life, but the course to its fulfillment.

31. Make it your moment-to-moment aim to recognize the difference between *being aware* of your thoughts, and *being carried along* by them.

32. Stop looking to the temporary for a sense of permanence.

33. Nothing is more useful, or practical, than the awakened awareness of the Free Mind.

34. Knowing without thinking is as natural as smiling without wanting anything from anyone.

35. You can have no destiny any higher, or happier, than your own nature.

36. Always look twice at any painful situation to see if what you saw the first time wasn't what the me mind *wanted* you to see.

Higher Actions That Lead To A Happier Life

37. The clearer your understanding of higher principles, the greater your personal possibility of harnessing their power.

38. Always make it your first choice to see what you can see about yourself and not what you can tell someone else about what's wrong with him or her.

39. All self pity is negative self fascination.

40. Consciously reject any thought or feeling that wants you to believe that you can't go beyond the you that you've always known.

41. An agitated mind can't correct itself, let alone the person or circumstance it calls into account for its crazed condition.

42. Self command is not won by overpowering our problems, but in seeing through the contradictions in our own consciousness that steal our natural powers of self possession.

43. Pretending you're not afraid works as long as nothing comes along and scares you!

44. Come awake as often as you can and bring yourself into the protective custody of the present moment.

45. Resisting any punishing inner state can never lead to its satisfactory resolution because no opposite has the power to cancel itself.

46. Any conflict is always first a question of consciousness.

47. You can be just as free as you're willing to see where you may be standing in your own way.

48. Think of the facts you can gather about the nature of the present moment as special anchors that will increasingly give you the power to remain there.

The Freedom You Want Also Wants You To Be Free

49. Awareness of the conflict inherent in the me mind's self compromising nature negates our involvement and unconscious identification with this divided level of mind.

50. To see the right place to begin, start this very moment to stand up to those parts of yourself that are afraid to come to a stop.

51. The only power to change where you're going in life rests within *knowing where you are*.

52. Without taking higher actions, plans for freeing yourself are just gold-plated weights.

53. By learning to look at each step we take as the whole of our journey, our attention is profitably focused on *where we are*, instead of on where we *think* we're going.

54. Knowing that nothing in the world can stop you from starting all over again in the right place is the same as having no fear of making a mistake.

55. The Free Mind knows that attention is prevention.

56. The starting place for going spiritually farther than you've ever gone before only comes into existence each time you reach and voluntarily dare to remain at that point where you're certain you can go no further.

57. Lose interest in holding on to any feeling of loss.

58. Spend everyday casual, but industrious; every moment alert, but relaxed.

59. Anybody can do what everybody else does; you do more.

60. Living from the Free Mind is a series of moment-to-moment victories.

A PERSONAL INVITATION AND SPECIAL OFFER FROM THE AUTHOR

Guy Finley lives and teaches in southern Oregon. You are invited to write to him with your questions or comments about any of the ideas in this book.

For information on additional books, booklets, tapes, and a schedule of ongoing classes in your area write to:

Guy Finley
Life Of Learning Foundation
P.O. Box 170 F
Merlin, Oregon 97532

Enclose a self addressed, stamped envelope (#10, legal size) and receive a free poster, "10 Secret Ways Higher Self Studies Help You Succeed In Life."

Stay in Touch. . .

Llewellyn publishes hundreds of books on your favorite subjects

Order by Phone

Call toll-free within the U.S. and Canada, **1–800–THE MOON**.
In Minnesota call **(612) 291–1970**.
We accept Visa, MasterCard, and American Express.

Order by Mail

Send the full price of your order (MN residents add 7% sales tax) in U.S. funds to:

**Llewellyn Worldwide
P.O. Box 64383, Dept. L217-9
St. Paul, MN 55164–0383, U.S.A.**

Postage and Handling

(for the U.S., Canada, and Mexico)

- ◆ $4.00 for orders $15.00 and under
- ◆ $5.00 for orders over $15.00
- ◆ No charge for orders over $100.00

We ship UPS in the continental United States. We ship standard mail to P.O. boxes. Orders shipped to Alaska, Hawaii, The Virgin Island, and Puerto Rico are sent first-class mail.

Orders shipped to Canada and Mexico are sent surface mail.

International orders: Airmail—add freight equal to price of each book to the total price of order, plus $5.00 for each non-book item (audiotapes, etc.). Surface mail—Add $1.00 per item.

Allow 4–6 weeks delivery on all orders. Postage and handling rates subject to change.

Group Discounts

We offer a 20% quantity discount to group leaders or agents. You must order a minimum of 5 copies of the same book to get our special quantity price.

Free Catalog

Get a free copy of our color catalog, *New Worlds of Mind and Spirit*. Subscribe for just $10.00 in the United States and Canada ($30.00 overseas, airmail). Many bookstores carry *New Worlds*—ask for it!

DESIGNING YOUR OWN DESTINY
The Power to Shape Your Future
Guy Finley

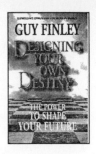

This book is for those who are ready for a book on self-transformation with principles that actually *work*. *Designing Your Own Destiny* is a practical, powerful guide that tells you, in plain language, exactly what you need to do to fundamentally change yourself and your life for the better, permanently.

Eleven powerful inner life exercises will show you how to master the strong and subtle forces that actually determine your life choices and your destiny. You'll discover why so many of your daily choices up to this point have been made by default, and how embracing the truth about yourself will banish your self-defeating behaviors forever. Everything you need for spiritual success is revealed in this book. Guy Finley reveals and removes many would-be roadblocks to your inner transformation, telling you how to dismiss fear, cancel self-wrecking resentment, stop secret self-sabotage and stop blaming others for the way you feel.

After reading *Designing Your Own Destiny*, you'll understand why you are perfectly equal to every task you set for yourself, and that you truly *can* change your life for the better!

1-56718-278-X, 160 pp., mass market, softcover **$6.99**

THE SECRET OF LETTING GO
Guy Finley

Whether you need to let go of a painful heartache, a destructive habit, a frightening worry or a nagging discontent, *The Secret of Letting Go* shows you how to call upon your own hidden powers and how they can take you through and beyond any challenge or problem. This book reveals the secret source of a brand-new kind of inner strength.

With a foreword by Desi Arnaz Jr., and introduction by Dr. Jesse Freeland, *The Secret of Letting Go* is a pleasing balance of questions and answers, illustrative examples, truth tales, and stimulating dialogues that allow the reader to share in the exciting discoveries that lead up to lasting self-liberation.

This is a book for the discriminating, intelligent, and sensitive reader who is looking for *real* answers.

0-87542-223-3, 240 pp., 5¼ x 8, softcover **$9.95**

To order, call 1–800–THE MOON
Prices subject to change without notice